TRUE STORIES
about THE PASSION

BOOKS

True Stories of the Passion

Copyright © 2005 O Books
An imprint of John Hunt Publishing Ltd., The Bothy, Deershot
Lodge, Park Lane, Ropley, Hants, SO24 0BE, UK
office@johnhunt-publishing.com
www.o-books.net

USA and Canada
NBN
custserv@nbnbooks.com
Tel: 1 800 462 6420 Fax: 1 800 338 4550

Australia
Brumby Books
sales@brumbybooks.com
Tel: 61 3 9761 5535 Fax: 61 3 9761 7095

New Zealand
Peaceful Living
books@peaceful-living.co.nz
Tel: 64 7 57 18105 Fax: 64 7 57 18513

Singapore
STP
davidbuckland@tlp.com.sg
Tel: 65 6276 Fax: 65 6276 7119

South Africa
Alternative Books
altbook@global.co.za
Tel: 27 011 792 7730 Fax: 27 011 972 7787

Design by Andrew Milne Design Ltd

ISBN 1 905047 36 3

A CIP catalogue record for this book is available
from the British Library.

Printed by Maple-Vail Book Manufacturing Group, USA

CONTENTS

Other books in this series include:

True Stories of Conversion

True Stories about The Bible

— *Part 1* —

STORIES *about* THE MEANING OF JESUS' PASSION

The shortest sermon

No words

It was probably the shortest sermon on record. That's because no words were spoken. It happened in the Middle Ages.

> **LIGHT from the BIBLE**
>
> *"Now Thomas . . . said to them, 'Unless I see the nail marks in his hands and put my finger where the nails were, and put my hand into his side, I will not believe it.' . . . Jesus came and stood among them . . . he said to Thomas, 'Put your finger here; see my hands. Reach out your hand and put it into my side. Stop doubting and believe.'"*
>
> JOHN 20:24-27

During Holy Week

One night when the congregation gathered to hear the preacher preach, he did not open his mouth. Instead he lit a lantern.

Then he set up a ladder to one side of a large crucifix. With lantern in hand, he climbed the ladder. He raised the lantern to show one of Christ's hands.

Then he climbed down, and moved the ladder to the other side. Again, he climbed the ladder. Again, he raised the lantern. And he showed the other hand of Christ.

That was the sermon.

Quotation to ponder

"Only once did God choose a completely sinless preacher."

ALEXANDER WHYTE

Pepita the poor gypsy girl

A beautiful model

Pepita was a poor gipsy girl. One day the famous Dusseldorf artist, Stenburg, saw her and realized that she would make a beautiful model. On her first visit to his studio she was amazed by the sight of his many paintings. Her eye was caught by an unfinished picture of the crucifixion, which Stenburg had been commissioned to paint by the wealthy church of St. Jerome.

"Who is that?" asked the girl, pointing to the most prominent figure.

"The Christ," answered Stenburg carelessly.

"What is being done to him?" she asked.

> **LIGHT *from* the BIBLE**
>
> *"He was despised and rejected by men . . ."*
>
> ISAIAH 53:3

"He is being crucified," the artist replied impatiently. "Who are those people around him – those with the bad faces?" asked Pepita.

"Now, look here," said the painter. "I can't talk to you! You must stand still and not ask questions."

"Was he very bad?"

The girl didn't dare to speak again, but she gazed and wondered. She was fascinated by the picture of the Christ and was unable to get it out of her thoughts. Then one day she ventured to ask: "Why did they crucify him? Was he bad – very bad?"

"No, very good," replied Stenburg.

That answer made Pepita even more curious, but she did not pluck up courage to ask her next question until the following day: "If he was so good, why did they crucify him?"

The eager, questioning face moved the artist. "Listen. I will tell you once and for all, and then you must ask no more questions." He proceeded to tell her the story of Jesus' crucifixion. This was new to Pepita, but so old to the artist that it had ceased to touch him. He could paint that dying agony without being moved, but the thought of it deeply moved Pepita's heart. She sighed and reverently gazed on the bleeding, agonizing picture of the suffering Christ.

Hymn to ponder

*The cross is the way
    of the lost
The cross is the staff
    of the lame
The cross is the guide
    of the blind
The cross is the strength
    of the weak
The cross is the hope
    of the hopeless
The cross is the freedom
    of the slaves
The cross is the water
    of the seeds
The cross is the
    consolation of the
    enslaved laborers
The cross is the source
    of those who seek water
The cross is the cloth
    of the naked.*

10TH-CENTURY AFRICAN HYMN

Artists and the cross of Jesus

It is little wonder that the crucifixion of Christ has been depicted by so many artists through the centuries. Artists have been fascinated by the

scene of Jesus dying outside the walls of Jerusalem, on a hill, between two criminals.

Pepita's last visit

When Pepita came to the studio for the last time, she said: "Signor, you must love him very much, do you not, when he has done all that for you?"

Stenburg's face flushed crimson. He was ashamed and turned away. Her plaintive words, however, continued to ring in his heart, disturbing and distressing him day and night.

"I can paint"

Some months later a large crowd trooped into the house of a poor person near the city walls. When Stenburg asked who they were, he was told, "A pack of interfering reformers." His curiosity got the better of him, and he went into the house. This resulted in his conversion to Christ. He found what he had longed for – a living faith. He now longed to share this good news about redemption through Christ's death and to tell everyone about Jesus' wonderful love. "But," he said to himself, "I cannot speak. If I tried, I could never articulate what I want to say. It burns in my heart, but I cannot express it, but I can paint!" He fell to his knees and asked God to help him to paint in a worthy way. His prayer was answered, and he produced a painting of the crucifixion that touched the hearts and lives of many people.

Hymn to ponder

*O sacred Head, once
  wounded,
With grief and pain
  weighed down,
How scornfully
  surrounded
With thorns, Thine
  only crown;
How pale art Thou
  with anguish,
With sore abuse and
  scorn!
How does that visage
  languish,
Which once was
  bright as morn!*

BERNARD OF CLAIRVAUX

The Dusseldorf gallery

Stenburg decided that he would not sell his precious painting. He presented it to his own city of Dusseldorf, to be displayed in the public gallery. There the people of Dusseldorf and visitors from all over the world flocked to see it. Voices were hushed and hearts melted as they stood before it and pondered the words written so distinctly beneath it: "All this I did for thee; What hast thou done for Me?"

LIGHT *from* the BIBLE

"And the keeper of the prison awaking out of his sleep, and seeing the prison doors open, he drew out his sword, and would have killed himself, supposing that the prisoners had been fled. But Paul cried with a loud voice, saying, 'Do thyself no harm: for we are all here.' Then he called for a light, and sprang in, and came trembling, and fell down before Paul and Silas, . . . and said, 'Sirs, what must I do to be saved?' And they said, 'Believe on the Lord Jesus Christ, and thou shalt be saved, and thy house.'"

ACTS 16:27-29 KJV

A poor weeping girl

Stenburg himself used to go the Dusseldorf gallery, watching from an obscure corner, as the people came to look at his picture. He prayed that God would bless the painted sermon. One day he noticed a poor girl weeping bitterly in front of it. He went to her. It was Pepita, his gipsy model. "Oh, Signor, if only he had loved me so!" she said. "I am only a poor gipsy. For you there is love, but not for such as I." And she burst into tears again.

"Pepita, it was also for you," explained the artist. He was now only too eager to answer all her questions. He told her about the wonderful life, sacrificial death, and amazing resurrection of Jesus. Pepita listened and believed, and she received the Lord Jesus Christ into her heart, there and then.

A gipsy encampment

Two years later, while Stenburg was comfortably seated in his home in front of blazing pine logs on a bitterly cold night, his servant showed in a man who had asked to see him urgently. Stenburg followed this stranger through the night to a clearing in the forest where there was a gipsy encampment. There, in a tent lit by the light of the moon, he found Pepita. Her face was pinched and hollow. She was dying.

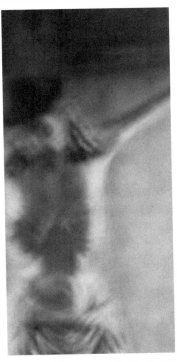

At the sound of the artist's voice she opened her eyes and said, "He has come for me! He holds out his hands! They are bleeding! And he says: 'For thee. All for you. All this I did for you.'" She lay still for a moment, and then she died.

Quotation to ponder

"God will spare the sinner because he did not spare his Son."

C. H. SPURGEON

Stenburg's painting and Count Zinzendorf

Count Zinzendorf

*T*hough the Baptist missionary William Carey is often referred to as the "Father of Modern Missions," he himself would credit Zinzendorf with that role, for he often referred to the model of the earlier Moravians in his journal.

LIGHT *from the* BIBLE

"Saying with a loud voice, Worthy is the Lamb that was slain to receive power, and riches, and wisdom, and strength, and honor, and glory, and blessing."

REVELATION 5:12 KJV

A young nobleman

Many years after Stenburg's death a young nobleman drove into Dusseldorf in his splendid carriage. While his horses were being watered and fed at an inn, he wandered into the famous picture gallery. He was rich, young, and intelligent, and the world lay at his feet, with all its treasures within his grasp.

Transfixed

But he stood in front of Stenburg's picture, transfixed. He read and re-read the words beneath it. He could not tear himself away. The love of Christ gripped his soul. Hours passed by, the light faded and the curator had to touch the weeping nobleman's shoulder and tell him that the gallery was closing. Night had come, but for this young man it was dawn.

He was Count Zinzendorf. He returned to the inn and went back to Paris in his carriage. From that moment he threw his life, fortune, and fame at the feet of the One who had spoken to his heart in that gallery.

Destroyed by fire
Stenburg's picture is no longer in the gallery at Dusseldorf, as both gallery and picture were destroyed in a fire. But the picture had preached, and God had used it to speak about his Son, Jesus Christ.

The meaning behind this painting never left Zinzendorf and his missionary work. He once summed up his evangelistic activities when he said: "Our method of proclaiming salvation is to point everyone to the loving Lamb, who died for us, offering Himself for our sins."

Quotation to ponder

"Do you think it was self-denial for the Lord Jesus to come down from heaven to rescue a world? Was it self-denial? No. It was love – love that swallows up everything, and first of all self."

NICOLAS LUDWIG VON ZINZENDORF,
SPEAKING TO JOHN WESLEY

Bamboo

A beautiful garden

Once upon a time, in the heart of an ancient Kingdom, there was a beautiful garden. And there, in the cool of the day, the Master of the garden would walk. Of all the plants of the garden, the most beautiful and most beloved was a gracious and noble bamboo.

Year after year, bamboo grew yet more noble and gracious, conscious of his Master's love and watchful delight, but modest and gentle. And often when the wind came to the garden, Bamboo would dance and play, tossing and swaying and leaping and bowing in joyful abandon, leading the Great Dance of the garden, which most delighted the Master's heart.

Shocking news

One day, the Master himself drew near to contemplate his Bamboo with eyes of curious expectancy. And Bamboo, in a passion of adoration, bowed his great head to the ground in loving greeting.

The Master spoke: "Bamboo, Bamboo, I would use you."

16

Bamboo flung his head to the sky in utter delight. The day of days had come, the day for which he had been made, the day to which he had been growing hour by hour, the day in which he would find his completion and his destiny.

His voice came low: "Master, I'm ready. Use me as you wish."

"Bamboo," The Master's voice was grave "I would have to take you and cut you down!"

> ## LIGHT *from the* BIBLE
>
> *"We are going up to Jerusalem, and the Son of Man will be betrayed to the chief priests and the teachers of the law. They will condemn him to death and will turn him over to the Gentiles to be mocked and flogged and crucified. On the third day he will be raised to life!"*
>
> MATTHEW 20:18-19

Horror of horrors

A trembling of great horror shook Bamboo. "Cut me down? Me, whom you, Master, has made the most beautiful in all thy Garden. Cut me down! Ah, not that. Not that. Use me for the joy, use me for the glory, oh master, but do not cut me down!"

"Beloved Bamboo," The Master's voice grew graver still "If I do not cut you down, I cannot use you."

Quotation to ponder

"The cross saves."

J. I. PACKER

Self-giving

The garden grew still. Wind held his breath. Bamboo slowly bent his proud and glorious head.

There was a whisper: "Master, if you cannot use me other than to cut me down then do your will and cut."

Total sacrifice

"Bamboo, beloved Bamboo, I would cut your leaves and branches from you also."

"Master, spare me. Cut me down and lay my beauty in the dust; but would you also have to take from me my leaves and branches too?"

"Bamboo, if I do not cut them away, I cannot use you."

The Sun hid his face.

A listening butterfly glided fearfully away. And Bamboo shivered in terrible expectancy, whispering low: "Master, cut away."

Death

"Bamboo, Bamboo," continued the Master, "I would yet split you in two and cut out your heart, for if I cut not so, I cannot use you."

Then Bamboo bowed to the ground: "Master, Master then cut and split."

So the Master of the garden took Bamboo and cut him down and hacked off his branches and stripped off his leaves and split him in two and cut out his heart.

A channel

And lifting him gently, the Master carried Bamboo to where there was a spring of fresh sparkling water in the midst of his dry fields. Then putting one end of the broken Bamboo in the spring and the other end into the water channel in the field, the Master gently laid down his beloved Bamboo.

> ### Hymn to ponder
>
> *Hold thou thy cross*
> *before my closing eyes;*
> *Shine through the gloom,*
> *and point me to the skies;*
> *Heaven's morning breaks,*
> *and earth's vain*
> *shadows flee;*
> *In life, in death, O Lord,*
> *abide with me.*
>
> HENRY FRANCIS LYTE

And the spring sang welcome, and the clear sparkling waters raced joyously down the channel of bamboo's torn body into the waiting fields. Then the rice was planted, and the days went by, and the shoots grew and the harvest came.

In that day Bamboo, once so glorious in his stately beauty, was yet more glorious in his brokenness and humility. For in his beauty he was life abundant, but in his brokenness he became a channel of abundant life to his Master's world.

LIGHT *from the* BIBLE

"I tell you the truth, unless a kernel of wheat falls to the ground and dies, it remains only a single seed. But if it dies, it produces many seeds."

JOHN 12:24

The birdcage

Easter Sunday morning

On Easter Sunday morning, George Thomas, a pastor in a small New England town, came to the church carrying a rusty, bent, old birdcage. He placed it beside the pulpit. Several eyebrows were raised and, as if in response, Pastor Thomas began to speak.

Three little wild birds

"I was walking through town yesterday when I saw a young boy coming toward me, swinging this birdcage. On the bottom of the cage were three little wild birds, shivering with cold and fright.

I stopped the boy and asked, 'What you got there, son?'

"Just some old birds," came the reply.

"What are you gonna do with them?" I asked.

"Take 'em home and have fun with 'em. I'm gonna tease 'em and pull out their feathers to make 'em fight. I'm gonna have a real good time."

"But you'll get tired of those birds sooner or later. What will you do then?"

"Oh, I got some cats. They like birds. I'll take 'em to them."

> ### LIGHT *from the* BIBLE
>
> *"I am the gate; whoever enters through me will be saved. He will come in and go out, and find pasture. The thief comes only to steal and kill and destroy; I have come that they may have life, and have it to the full."*
>
> JOHN 10:9-10

"How much?"

The pastor was silent for a moment. "How much do you want for those birds, son?"

"Huh? Why, you don't want them birds, mister. They're just plain old field birds. They don't sing – they ain't even pretty!"

"How much?"

The boy sized up the pastor as if he were crazy and said, "$10?"

Quotation to ponder

"The symbol of the cross in the church points to the God who was crucified not between two candles on an altar, but between two thieves in the place of the skull, where the outcasts belong, outside the gates of the city."

JURGEN MOLTMANN

LIGHT *from the* BIBLE

"At that moment the curtain of the temple was torn in two from top to bottom. The earth shook and the rocks split. The tombs broke open and the bodies of many holy people who had died were raised to life. They came out of the tombs, and after Jesus' resurrection they went into the holy city and appeared to many people."

MATTHEW 27:51-53

Set them free

The pastor reached in his pocket and took out a ten-dollar note. He placed it in the boy's hand. In a flash, the boy was gone. The pastor picked up the cage and gently carried it to the end of the alley where there was a tree and a grassy spot.

Setting the cage down, he opened the door, and by softly tapping the bars persuaded the birds out, setting them free . . .

Well, that explained the empty birdcage on the pulpit, and then the pastor began to tell this story.

The pastor's story

One day Satan and Jesus were having a conversation. Satan had just come from the Garden of Eden, and he was gloating and boasting. "Yes, sir, I just caught the world full of people down there. Set me a trap, used bait I knew they couldn't resist. Got 'em all!"

"What are you going to do with them?" Jesus asked.

"Oh, I'm gonna have fun! I'm gonna teach them how to marry and divorce each other. How to hate and abuse each other. How to drink and smoke and curse. How to invent guns and bombs and kill each other. I'm really gonna have fun!"

"And what will you do when you get done with them?" Jesus asked.

"Oh, I'll kill 'em."

"How much?"

"How much do you want for them?"

"Oh, you don't want those people. They ain't no good. Why, you'll take them and they'll just hate you. They'll spit on you, curse you, and kill you!! You don't want those people!!"

"How much?"

Satan looked at Jesus and sneered, "All your tears, and all your blood. Your life."

Jesus paid the price.

> ## Quotation to ponder
>
> *"In the cross is health,*
> *in the cross is life,*
> *in the cross is protection*
> *   from enemies,*
> *in the cross is heavenly*
> *   sweetness,*
> *in the cross strength of mind,*
> *in the cross joy of the Spirit,*
> *in the cross the height of*
> *   virtue,*
> *in the cross perfection of*
> *   holiness."*
>
> THOMAS À KEMPIS

The pastor picked up the cage, opened the door and he walked from the pulpit.

Death row

A following letter was written to a man on death row by the father of the man whom the man on death row had killed.

The letter

You are probably surprised that I, of all people, am writing a letter to you, but I ask you to read it in its  entirety and consider its request seriously.

As the Father of the man whom you took part in murdering, I have something very important to say to you.

I forgive you. With all my heart, I forgive you. I realize it may be hard for you to believe, but I really do.

At your trial, when you confessed to your part in the events that cost my Son his life and asked for my forgiveness, I immediately granted you that forgiving love from my heart. I can only hope you believe me and will accept my forgiveness. But this is not all I have to say to you.

An offer

I want to make you an offer – I want you to become my adopted child. You see, my Son who died was my only child, and I now want to share my life with you and leave my riches to you.

Freed

This may not make sense to you or anyone else, but I believe you are worth the offer. I have arranged matters so that if you will receive my offer of forgiveness, not only will you be pardoned for your crime, but you also will be set free from your imprisonment, and your sentence of death will be dismissed.

Adopted

At that point, you will become my adopted child and heir to all my riches.

> ### LIGHT from the BIBLE
>
> *"The LORD is compassionate and gracious,*
> *slow to anger, abounding in love.*
> *He will not always accuse, nor will he harbor his anger forever;*
> *he does not treat us as our sins deserve*
> *or repay us according to our iniquities.*
> *For as high as the heavens are above the earth,*
> *so great is his love for those who fear him;*
> *as far as the east is from the west,*
> *so far has he removed our transgressions from us."*
>
> PSALM 103:8-12

I realize this is a risky offer for me to make to you – you might be tempted to reject my offer completely – but I make it to you without reservation. Also, I realize it may seem foolish to make such an offer to one who cost my Son his life, but I now have a great love and an unchangeable forgiveness in my heart for you.

An heir

Finally, you may be concerned that once you accept my offer you may do something to cause you to be denied your rights as an heir to my wealth. Nothing could be further from the truth. If I can forgive you for your part in my Son's death, I can forgive you for anything. I know you never will be perfect, but you do not have to be perfect to receive my offer. Besides, I believe that once you have accepted my offer and begin to experience the riches that will come to you from me, that your primary response will be gratitude and loyalty.

Some would call me foolish for my offer to you, but I wish for you to call me your Father.

Sincerely, the Father of Jesus

LIGHT *from the* BIBLE

"As for you, you were dead in your transgressions and sins, in which you used to live when you followed the ways of this world and of the ruler of the kingdom of the air, the spirit who is now at work in those who are disobedient."

EPHESIANS 2:1-2

Quotation to ponder

"Christ was delivered for our sins that we might be delivered from our sins."

C. H. SPURGEON

Hymn to ponder

We may not know, we cannot tell,
What pains He had to bear;
But we believe it was for us
He hung and suffered there.

He died that we might be forgiven,
He died to make us good,
That we might go at last to Heav'n,
Saved by His precious blood.

There was no other good enough
To pay the price of sin;
He only could unlock the gate
Of heaven and let us in.

O dearly, dearly has He loved,
And we must love Him, too,
And trust in His redeeming blood,
And try His works to do.

CECIL F. ALEXANDER

Donuts

Steve

A boy called Steve attended school in Utah. Brother Christianson taught at this particular school. He had an open-door policy and would take in any student that had been thrown out of another class as long as they would abide by his rules. Steve had been kicked out of his sixth period and no other teacher wanted him, so he went into Brother Christianson's class.

Steve was told that he could not be late, so he arrived just seconds before the bell rang and he would sit in the very back of the room. He would also be the first to leave after the class was over.

> **LIGHT from the BIBLE**
>
> *"And when Jesus had cried out again in a loud voice, he gave up his spirit."*
>
> MATTHEW 27:50

The challenge

One day, Brother Christianson asked Steve to stay after class so he could talk with him. After class, Brother Christianson pulled Steve aside and said, "You think you're pretty tough, don't you?"

Steve's answer was, "Yeah, I do."

Then Brother Christianson asked, "How many push-ups can you do?"

Steve said, "I do about two hundred every night."

"Two hundred? That's pretty good, Steve," Brother

Christianson said. "Do you think you could do three hundred?"

Steve replied, "I don't know. I've never done three hundred at one time."

"Do you think you could?" asked Brother Christianson again.

"Well, I can try," said Steve.

Challenge accepted

"Can you do three hundred in sets of ten? I need you to do three hundred in sets of ten for this to work. Can you do it? I need you to tell me you can do it," Brother Christianson insisted.

Steve said, "Well, I think I can. Yeah, I can do it." Brother Christianson said, "Good! I need you to do this on Friday."

Big donuts

Friday came and Steve got to class early and sat in the front of the room. When class started, Brother Christianson pulled out a big box of donuts. Now these weren't the normal kinds of donuts, they were the extra fancy, big, kind, with cream centers and frosting swirls.

Quotation to ponder

"Christianity is not a decision for Christ, but a complete surrender to let Christ take the lordship."

OSWALD CHAMBERS

Everyone was pretty excited – it was Friday, the last class of the day, and they were going to get an early start on the weekend.

Ten push-ups per donut

Brother Christianson went to the first girl in the first row and asked, "Cynthia, do you want a donut?" Cynthia said, "Yes."

Brother Christianson then turned to Steve and asked, "Steve, would you do ten push-ups so that Cynthia can have a donut?"

Steve said, "Sure," and jumped down from his desk to do a quick ten. Then Steve again sat in his desk. Brother Christianson put a donut on Cynthia's desk.

Joe

Brother Christianson then went to Joe, the next person, and asked, "Joe do you want a donut?"

Joe said, "Yes."

Brother Christianson asked, "Steve would you do ten

> *Quotations to ponder*
>
> *"The entrance fee into the kingdom of heaven is nothing: the annual subscription is everything."*
>
> HENRY DRUMMOND

LIGHT *from the* **BIBLE**

"With a loud cry, Jesus breathed his last."

MARK 15:37

push-ups so Joe can have a donut?"

Steve did ten push-ups, Joe got a donut.

And so it went, down the first aisle, Steve did ten push-ups for every person before they got their donut.

Scott

And down the second aisle, till Brother Christianson came to Scott.

Scott was captain of the football team and center of the basketball team. He was very popular and never lacking for female companionship. When Brother Christianson asked, "Scott do you want a donut?" Scott's reply was, "Well, can I do my own push-ups?"

Brother Christianson said, "No, Steve has to do them."

Then Scott said, "Well, I don't want one then."

Brother Christianson then turned to Steve and asked, "Steve, would you do ten push-ups so Scott can have a donut he doesn't want?" Steve started to do ten push-ups.

Scott said, "Hey! I said I didn't want one!"

Brother Christianson said, "Look, this is my classroom, my class, my desks, and my donuts. Just leave it on the desk if you don't want it." And he put a donut on Scott's desk.

> **LIGHT** *from the* **BIBLE**
>
> *"Jesus called out with a loud voice, 'Father, into your hands I commit my spirit.' When he had said this, he breathed his last."*
>
> LUKE 23:46

31

The third row

Now by this time, Steve had begun to slow down a little. He just stayed on the floor between sets because it took too much effort to be getting up and down. You could start to see a little perspiration coming out around his brow.

Brother Christianson started down the third row. Now the students were beginning to get a little angry.

Jenny

Brother Christianson asked Jenny, "Jenny, do you want a donut?"

Jenny said, "No."

Then Brother Christianson asked Steve, "Steve, would you do ten push-ups so Jenny can have a donut that she doesn't want?" Steve did ten, Jenny got a donut.

> ### LIGHT *from the* BIBLE
>
> *"When he had received the drink, Jesus said, 'It is finished.' With that, he bowed his head and gave up his spirit."*
>
> JOHN 19:30

By now, the students were beginning to say "no" and there were all these uneaten donuts on the desks. Steve was also having to put a great deal of effort to get these push-ups done for each donut. A small pool of sweat appeared on the floor beneath his face, his arms and brow were beginning to get red because of the physical effort involved.

Quotation to ponder

"Your intellect says, 'I accept Christ,' your emotions say, 'I love Christ,' and your will says 'I will follow Christ.'"

BILLY GRAHAM

Thirty-four students

Brother Christianson asked Robert to watch Steve to make sure he did ten push-ups in a set because he couldn't bear to watch all of Steve's work for all of those uneaten donuts. So Robert began to watch Steve closely. Brother Christianson started down the fourth row. During his class, however, some students had wandered in and sat along the heaters along the sides of the room. When Brother Christianson realized this, he did a quick count and saw thirty-four students in the room. He started to worry if Steve would be able to make it.

Brother Christianson went on to the next person and the next and the next. Near the end of that row, Steve was really having a rough time. He was taking a lot more time to complete each set.

Steve asked Brother Christianson, "Do I have to make my nose touch on each one?"

Brother Christianson thought for a moment, "Well, they're your push-ups. You can do them any way that you want."

And Brother Christianson went on.

Enter Jason

A few moments later, Jason came to the room and was about to come in when all the students yelled, "No! Don't come in! Stay out!" Jason didn't know what was going on.

Steve picked up his head and said, "No, let him come."

Brother Christianson said, "You realize that if Jason comes in you will have to do ten push-ups for him."

> ## Quotation to ponder
>
> *"The New Testament definition of a Christian is a person 'in Christ.'"*
>
> JOHN R. W. STOTT

Steve said, "Yes, let him come in."

Brother Christianson said, "Okay, I'll let you get Jason's out of the way right now. Jason, do you want a donut?"

"Yes."

"Steve, will you do ten push-ups so that Jason can have a donut?"

Steve did ten push-ups very slowly and with great effort. Jason, bewildered, was handed a donut and sat down.

Popular cheerleaders

Brother Christianson finished the fourth row, then started on those seated on the heaters. Steve's arms were now shaking with each push-up in a struggle to lift himself against the force of gravity. Sweat was dropping off of his face and, by this time, there was not a dry eye in the room.

The very last two girls in the room were cheerleaders and very popular. Brother Christianson went to Linda, the second to last, and asked, "Linda, do you want a doughnut?"

Linda said, very sadly, "No, thank you."

Brother Christianson asked Steve, "Steve, would you do ten push-ups so that Linda can have a donut she doesn't want?" Grunting from the effort, Steve did ten very slow push-ups for Linda.

Then Brother Christianson turned to the last girl, Susan. "Susan, do you want a donut?"

Susan, with tears flowing down her face, asked, "Brother Christianson, can I help him?"

Brother Christianson, with tears of his own, said, "No, he has to do it alone. Steve, would you do ten push-ups so Susan can have a donut?"

As Steve very slowly finished his last push-up, with the understanding that he had accomplished all that was required of him, having done three hundred and seventy push-ups, his arms buckled beneath him and he fell to the floor.

Brother Christianson turned to the room and said. "And so it was, that our Savior, Jesus Christ, pleaded to the Father, 'Into thy hands I commend my spirit.' With the understanding that He had done everything that was required of Him, he collapsed on the cross and died. And like some of those in this room, many of us leave the gift on the desk, uneaten."

Full pardon

US Supreme Court

*S*eldom has a person under sentence of death refused a pardon. Yet there is one case on record, in the annals of the US Supreme Court, in which a man sentenced to die actually did refuse to accept a pardon.

Jackson and Porter

During the presidency of Andrew Jackson, George Wilson, a postal clerk, with Porter, his accomplice, robbed a federal payroll from a train and in the process killed a guard. The US Supreme Court records show that the two men, Wilson and Porter, were convicted

---

LIGHT *from the* BIBLE

"My dear children, I write this to you so that you will not sin. But if anybody does sin, we have one who speaks to the Father in our defense – Jesus Christ, the Righteous One. He is the atoning sacrifice for our sins, and not only for ours but also for the sins of the whole world. We know that we have come to know him if we obey his commands. The man who says, 'I know him,' but does not do what he commands is a liar, and the truth is not in him. But if anyone obeys his word, God's love is truly made complete in him. This is how we know we are in him: Whoever claims to live in him must walk as Jesus did."

1 JOHN 2:1-6

---

and sentenced to be hanged for robbery of the US mails in 1829.

Porter was executed on 2 July 1830. But because of public sentiment against capital punishment a movement began to secure a presidential pardon for Wilson.

About three weeks before Wilson's execution, he was granted a pardon by President Andrew Jackson. When he was given the opportunity to plead the pardon he refused to do so. Amazingly, Wilson insisted that he would not accept the pardon.

Pardon refused

Refusal to accept a pardon was a point of law that had never been raised before and the Supreme Court was called upon to give a decision. So in January 1833 the Supreme Court handed down the following decision, written by Chief Justice John Marshall.

Defining a pardon

"A pardon is an act of grace, proceeding from the power entrusted with the execution of the laws, which exempts the individual on whom it is bestowed, from the punishment the law inflicts for a crime he has committed. A pardon is a deed that has no value apart from that which the receiver gives to it. It may then be rejected by the person to whom it is tendered: and if it is rejected we have found no power in a Court to force it upon him. George Wilson has refused to accept the pardon. We cannot conceive why he would do so, but he has. Therefore, George Wilson must die."

The court's decision

Chief Justice John Marshall also handed down the court's decision: "As punishment for his crime, George Wilson, on a day appointed by the court, was taken from his cell and hanged to satisfy the requirements of the law. Pardon, declared the Supreme Court, must not only be granted, it must be accepted."

Delivery and acceptance

This was a most unusual case and most people would agree that Wilson was a fool for refusing to accept a pardon. In Justice Marshall's definition, "A pardon is

LIGHT *from the* BIBLE

"This is how God showed his love among us: He sent his one and only Son into the world that we might live through him. This is love: not that we loved God, but that he loved us and sent his Son as an atoning sacrifice for our sins."

1 JOHN 4:9-10

an act of grace" – a free, unmerited favor, unearned, which cannot be bought. The decision also reads that, "A pardon is a deed, to the validity of which delivery is essential, and delivery is not complete without acceptance."

Refusal

"In the case of real property a deed must be delivered and acknowledged before the transaction is complete. The Court extended this ruling to apply to a man's physical life. The Bible extends it to include his eternal soul. God executed his deed on Calvary, and sealed it in the blood of His Son, but the transaction is not complete in your case until you definitely accept Christ as your Savior Surety." S. E. Slocum

Quotation to ponder

"God has promised pardon to him who repents."

ANSELM

Giving blood

Orphans

It was a quiet morning in Korea. In a small valley, there was a little wooden building with a corrugated steel roof. It was an orphanage that housed many young children who had lost their parents in the war.

Suddenly, the quiet of the morning was

LIGHT from the BIBLE

"My command is this: Love each other as I have loved you. Greater love has no one than this, that he lay down his life for his friends. You are my friends if you do what I command."

JOHN 15:12-14

shattered when a mortar shell fell and landed squarely on top of the orphanage. The roof was ripped apart by the blast and pieces of steel roofing were blasted all through the orphanage wounding many of the children.

One little girl was hit in the leg by the flying metal and her leg was immediately amputated just below her knee. She was lying in the rubble of the orphanage quietly when they found her. A tourniquet was immediately applied and a runner was sent to the MASH hospital to fetch medical help for the children.

Urgent need for blood

When the doctors and nurses arrived, they began to attend to the wounded children. When the doctor saw the little girl, he realized that her greatest need at the moment was blood. He immediately called for records from the orphanage to find someone with her blood type. A nurse who could read and speak Korean began to call out the names of all the children with the same blood type as the little girl.

One boy volunteer

After a few minutes there was a group of wide-eyed children assembled. The doctor spoke to the group and the nurse translated, "Would one of you be willing to give this little girl your blood?"

The children looked shocked, but no one said a word. Again the doctor pleaded, "Please will one of you give her your blood, because if you don't, she is going to die!"

Finally a boy in the back raised his hand and the nurse laid him down on a bed to prepare him for the taking of his blood.

Quotation to ponder

"Jesus ventured – as no prophet had ever ventured – to proclaim God's forgiveness, completely gratis, instead of legal penalties, and also to grant it in a personal way in order by this very encouragement to make possible repentance and forgiveness towards our fellow-men."

HANS KÜNG

LIGHT *from the* BIBLE

"But now a righteousness from God, apart from law, has been made known, to which the Law and the Prophets testify. This righteousness from God comes through faith in Jesus Christ to all who believe. There is no difference, for all have sinned and fall short of the glory of God, and are justified freely by his grace through the redemption that came by Christ Jesus. God presented him as a sacrifice of atonement, through faith in his blood."

ROMANS 3:21-25

"Does it hurt?"

When the nurse asked for his arm in order to sterilize the skin, the boy began to whimper.

"Relax," she said, "It won't hurt."

When the doctor took his arm and inserted the needle, he began to cry.

"Does it hurt?" the doctor asked. But the boy only cried louder.

"I'm hurting him!" the doctor thought and he tried to ease his pain and comfort him, but to no avail.

Finally, after what seemed like a long time, the blood was drawn and the needle was removed. The little boy just laid and sobbed for a few minutes.

"Did it hurt?"

After the blood was given to the wounded girl and her condition was stabilized, the doctor was curious. He took the Korean-speaking nurse back over to the little boy and told the nurse to ask him, "Did it hurt?"

The boy said, "No, it did not hurt."

"Then why were you crying?" the doctor asked.

"Because I was afraid of dying," the boy said.

The doctor was stunned! "Why did you think you would die?"

With tears in his eyes the boy replied, "Because I thought that in order to save her you would have to take all of my blood!"

"I loved her"

The doctor didn't know what to say! Then he asked, "But if you thought that you were going to die, why did you offer to give her your blood?" With tears streaming down his face, he said, "Because she was my friend and I loved her!"

Quotation to ponder

"The blood of Christ may seem to be a grim, repulsive subject to those who do not realize its true significance, but to those who have accepted his redemption and have been set free from sin's chains, the blood of Christ is precious."

BILLY GRAHAM

The old man and the sea

A childhood friend

After a few of the usual Sunday evening hymns, the church's pastor once again slowly stood up, walked over to the pulpit, and gave a very brief introduction to his childhood friend.

With that, an elderly man stepped up to the pulpit to speak.

The choice

"A father, his son, and a friend of his son were sailing off the Pacific Coast," he began, "when a fast-approaching storm blocked any attempt to get back to shore. The waves were so high, that even though the father was an experienced sailor, he could not keep the boat upright, and the three were swept into the ocean."

The old man hesitated for a moment, making eye contact with two teenagers who were, for the first time since the service began, looking somewhat interested in his story.

He continued, "Grabbing a rescue line, the father had to make the most excruciating decision of his life to which boy he would throw the other end of the line.

LIGHT *from the* BIBLE

". . . who did not spare his own Son, but gave him up for us all – how will he not also, along with him, graciously give us all things?"

ROMANS 8:32

He only had seconds to make the decision.

"The father knew that his son was a Christian, and he also knew that his son's friend was not. The agony of his decision could not be matched by the torrent of waves. As the father yelled out, 'I love you, son!' he threw the line to his son's friend. By the time he pulled the friend back to the capsized boat, his son had disappeared into the raging waves of the sea. His body was never recovered."

> ## Quotation to ponder
>
> *"The cross is our tree of life."*
>
> VIC REASONER

Silence

By this time, the two teenagers were sitting straighter in the pew, waiting for the next words to come out of the old man's mouth.

"The father," he continued, "knew his son would step into eternity with Jesus, and he could not bear the thought of his son's friend stepping into an eternity without Jesus. Therefore, he sacrificed his son. How great is the love of God that He should do the same for us."

With that, the old man turned and sat back down in his chair as silence filled the room.

Unrealistic

Within minutes after the service ended, the two teenagers were at the old man's side. "That was a nice story," politely started one of the boys, "but I don't think it was very realistic for a father to give up his son's life in hopes that the other boy would become a Christian."

"Well, you've got a point there," the old man replied, glancing down at his worn Bible. A big smile broadened his narrow face, and he once again looked up at the boys and said, "It sure isn't very realistic, is it? But I'm standing here today to tell you that that story gives me a glimpse of what it must have been like for God to give up His Son for me."

"You see, I was that father and your pastor is my son's friend."

> **LIGHT from the BIBLE**
>
> *"And this is his command: to believe in the name of his Son, Jesus Christ, and to love one another as he commanded us."*
>
> 1 JOHN 3:23

Hymn to ponder

When I survey the wondrous cross
On which the Prince of glory died,
My richest gain I count but loss,
And pour contempt on all my pride.

Forbid it, Lord, that I should boast,
Save in the death of Christ my God!
All the vain things that charm me most,
I sacrifice them to His blood.

See from His head, His hands, His feet,
Sorrow and love flow mingled down!
Did e'er such love and sorrow meet,
Or thorns compose so rich a crown?

His dying crimson, like a robe,
Spreads o'er His body on the tree;
Then I am dead to all the globe,
And all the globe is dead to me.

Were the whole realm of nature mine,
That were a present far too small;
Love so amazing, so divine,
Demands my soul, my life, my all.

ISAAC WATTS
HENRY FRANCIS LYTE

Queen Victoria visits a paper mill

Rags

One day Queen Victoria visited a paper mill owned by one of her subjects, and the owner was happy to show her through the great plant, explaining in detail the different processes used to manufacture paper.

During the journey through the factory she was taken into a large room filled with rags. They were in bins, in bales, and in huge piles on the floor. Some of them had been brought in by rag-pickers and were filthy and dirty. These were being sorted and processed by the workmen.

Victoria's questions

"Do you make paper of these?" the queen inquired.

"Yes, our best paper is made from rags," the owner explained.

She seemed to be in deep thought, then revealed

Quotation to ponder

"We are told that Christ was killed for us, that His death has washed out our sins, and that by dying He disabled death itself. That is the formula. That is Christianity. That is what has to be believed."

C. S. LEWIS

what had been going through her mind. "But how can these dirty rags ever be made into clean white paper?"

"We have washes," the guide explained, "which remove all the dirt and grime. We have chemical processes too, Your Majesty, by which every bit of color is removed from even these red rags."

LIGHT *from the* BIBLE

"Do you not know that the wicked will not inherit the kingdom of God? Do not be deceived: Neither the sexually immoral nor idolaters nor adulterers nor male prostitutes nor homosexual offenders nor thieves nor the greedy nor drunkards nor slanderers nor swindlers will inherit the kingdom of God. And that is what some of you were. But you were washed, you were sanctified, you were justified in the name of the Lord Jesus Christ and by the Spirit of our God."

1 CORINTHIANS 6:9-11

A surprise

A few days later the queen was surprised to find on her desk a neatly wrapped parcel, which on opening she found contained some of the whitest, most beautiful paper she had ever seen. On each sheet were her name and a watermark of her likeness. There was also a note from the man who had shown her through the paper mill.

Hymn to ponder

Blessed assurance, Jesus is mine!
Oh what a foretaste of Glory Divine!
Heir of salvation, purchase of God,
Born of the Spirit, washed in His Blood.

FANNY CROSBY

> ## LIGHT *from the* BIBLE
>
> *"'Come now, let us reason together,' says the LORD. 'Though your sins are like scarlet, they shall be as white as snow; though they are red as crimson, they shall be like wool.'"*
>
> ISAIAH 1:18

The note

"Will the queen be pleased to accept a specimen of my paper, with the assurance that every sheet was manufactured from the rags which she saw in the warehouse on her recent visit to our plant, and I trust the result is such as even the queen may admire.

Will the queen also allow me to say that I have had many a good sermon preached to me in my mill?

I can understand how the Lord Jesus can take the poor sinner, and the vilest of the vile, and make them clean; and how though their sins be as scarlet, He can make them white as snow. And I can see how He can put His own name upon them: and just as these rags, transformed, may go into a royal palace and be admired, so poor sinners can be received into the palace of the Great King."

Diving surprise

Atheist diver

A young man who had been raised as an atheist was training to be an Olympic diver. The only religious influence in his life came from his outspoken Christian friend. The young diver never really paid much attention to his friend's sermons, but he heard them often.

LIGHT from the BIBLE

"When they had crucified him . . ."

MATTHEW 27:35

Cross-shaped shadow

One night the diver went to the indoor pool at the college he attended. The lights were all off, but as the pool had big skylights and the moon was bright, there was plenty of light to practice by.

The young man climbed up to the highest diving board and as he turned his back to the pool on the edge of the board and extended his arms out, he saw his shadow on the wall. The shadow of his body in the shape of a cross.

Drained

Instead of diving, he knelt down and asked God to come into his life. As the young man stood, a maintenance man walked in and turned the lights on. The pool had been drained for repairs.

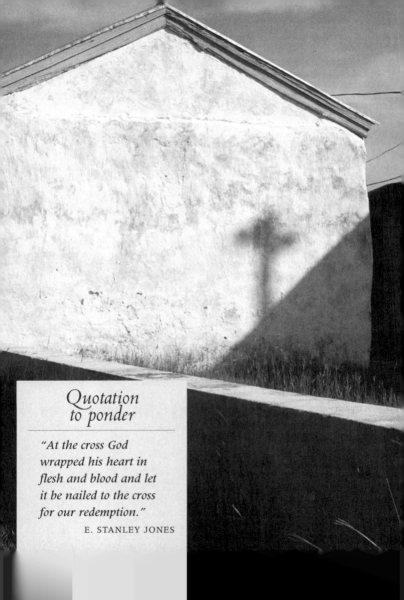

Quotation to ponder

"At the cross God wrapped his heart in flesh and blood and let it be nailed to the cross for our redemption."

E. STANLEY JONES

The old rugged cross

1913

In 1913, during the early years of his ministry, Rev. George Bennard was struggling with a problem that caused him much suffering. He was "praying for a full understanding of the cross and its plan in Christianity."

His mind went back again and again to Christ's anguish on the cross. He knew very well that this was the heart of the gospel. The cross he pictured was no gold-covered icon. It was a rough, full of splinters, and stained with blood.

> ### LIGHT *from* the BIBLE
>
> *"For God so loved the world that he gave his one and only Son, that whoever believes in him shall not perish but have eternal life."*
>
> JOHN 3:16

Consequently, he spent many hours in study, prayer, and meditation, until he could say, "I saw the Christ of the cross as if I were seeing John 3:16 leave the printed page, take form, and act out the meaning of redemption."

He struggled for weeks

This theme was so great, it needed a song. In a room in Albion, Michigan, Bennard sat down and wrote a tune. But the only words that would come to him were "I'll cherish the old rugged cross." He struggled for weeks to set words to the melody he had written.

Hymn to ponder

On a hill far away stood an old rugged cross,
The emblem of suffering and shame;
And I love that old cross where the dearest and best
For a world of lost sinners was slain.

REFRAIN
So I'll cherish the old rugged cross,
Till my trophies at last I lay down;
I will cling to the old rugged cross,
And exchange it some day for a crown.

GEORGE BENNARD, 1873–1958

The lines came

As a Methodist evangelist, Bennard was scheduled to preach a series of messages in New York. He found himself focusing on the cross. The theme of the cross grew increasingly more urgent to him. Back in Albion, Michigan, he sat down and tried again to put together the words. This time the lines came. He later told Dr. Al Smith, "I sat down and immediately was able to rewrite the stanzas of the song without so much as one word failing to fall into place. I called in my wife, took out my guitar, and sang the completed song to her. She was thrilled!"

Bennard's diary entry

"The inspiration came to me one day in 1913, when I

was staying in Albion, Michigan," wrote George Bennard about the composition of this hymn.

"I began to write The Old Rugged Cross. I completed the melody first. The words that I first wrote were imperfect. The words of the finished hymn were put into my heart in answer to my own need. Shortly thereafter it was introduced at special meetings in Pokagon, Michigan, on June 7, 1913."

The hymn was introduced to a large convention in Chicago, and its fame spread

> ### LIGHT *from* *the* BIBLE
>
> *"Pilate had a notice prepared and fastened to the cross. It read: JESUS OF NAZARETH, THE KING OF THE JEWS. Many of the Jews read this sign, for the place where Jesus was crucified was near the city, and the sign was written in Aramaic, Latin and Greek. The chief priests of the Jews protested to Pilate, 'Do not write "The King of the Jews," but that this man claimed to be king of the Jews.' Pilate answered, 'What I have written, I have written.'"*
>
> JOHN 19:19-22

rapidly throughout the Christian world. Before long this hymn became one of the top ten most popular hymns of the twentieth century.

Twelve-foot high cross
Today, a twelve-foot high wooden cross stands on a roadside near Reed City, Michigan, honoring the composer.

On it are the words "Old Rugged Cross." A sign reminds passersby that this is the "Home of Author, Rev. Geo. Bennard."

Hymn to ponder

O that old rugged cross, so despised by the world,
Has a wondrous attraction for me;
For the dear Lamb of God left His glory above
To bear it to dark Calvary.

In the old rugged cross, stained with blood so divine,
A wondrous beauty I see;
For 'twas on that old cross Jesus suffered and died,
To pardon and sanctify me.

To the old rugged cross, I will ever be true,
Its shame and reproach gladly bear;
Then He'll call me some day to my home far away,
Where His glory forever I'll share.

GEORGE BENNARD, 1873–1958

Paid in full

After-life courtroom scene

After living a decent life my time on earth came to an end.

The first thing I remember is sitting on a bench in the waiting room of what I thought to be a courthouse. The doors opened and I was instructed to come in and have a seat by the defense table.

As I looked around I saw the "prosecutor," he was a villainous looking gent who snarled as he stared at me, he definitely was the most evil person I have ever seen. I sat down and looked to my left and there sat my lawyer, a kind and gentle looking man whose appearance seemed very familiar to me.

> **LIGHT** *from*
> *the* **BIBLE**
>
> *"Forgive us our debts."*
> MATTHEW 6:12

The corner door flew open and there appeared the Judge in full flowing robes. He commanded an awesome presence as he moved across the room and I couldn't take my eyes off of him.

As he took his seat behind the bench he said, "Let us begin."

Satan

The prosecutor rose and said: "My name is Satan and I am here to show you why this man belongs in hell." He proceeded to tell of lies that I told, things that I stole and in the past when I cheated others. Satan spoke about other evil deeds I had committed during my life. The more he spoke the further down in my seat I sank. I was so embarrassed that I couldn't look at anyone, even my own lawyer, as the Devil told of sins that even I had completely forgotten about.

My representative sat silent

As upset as I was at Satan for telling all these things about me, I was equally upset at my representative who sat there silently not offering any form of defense at all. I know I had been guilty of those things, but I had done some good in my life – couldn't that at least equal out part of the harm I've done?

Hymn to ponder

Dear Lord and Father of
*   mankind,*
Forgive our foolish ways!
Reclothe us in our rightful
*   mind,*
In purer lives thy service find,
In deeper reverence, praise.

JOHN GREENLEAF WHITTIER

"He belongs in hell"

Satan finished with a fury and said, "This man belongs in hell, he is guilty of all that I have charged and there is not a person who can prove otherwise. Justice will finally be served this day."

My lawyer

When it was his turn, my lawyer first asked if he might approach the bench. The judge allowed this over the strong objection of Satan, and beckoned him to come forward.

As he got up and started walking I was able to see him now in his full splendor and majesty. Now I realized why he seemed so familiar, this was Jesus representing me, my Lord and my Savior.
He stopped at the bench and softly said to the judge, "Hi Dad."

"This man is guilty"

Then he turned to address the court. "Satan was correct in saying that this man had sinned, I won't deny any of these allegations. And yes the wages of sins is death and this man deserves to be punished."

Jesus took a deep breath and turned to his Father

with out-stretched arms and said, "However, I died on the cross so that this person might have eternal life and he has accepted me as his Savior, so he is mine." My Lord continued, and said, "His name is written in the book of life and no one can snatch him from me. Satan still does not understand. This man is to be given mercy. There is nothing else that needs to be done, I've done it all."

The Judge

As Jesus sat down, he quietly paused, and looked at his Father. The Judge lifted his mighty hand and spoke in a loud voice: "This man is free – the penalty for him has already been paid in full. Case dismissed."

Satan defeated

As my Lord led me away I could hear Satan ranting and raving, "I won't give up, I'll win the next one."

"Have you ever lost?"

I asked Jesus as he gave me my instructions where to go next, "Have you ever lost a case?"

Christ lovingly smiled and said, "Everyone who has come to me and asked me to represent them has received the same verdict as you, Paid in Full."

> **LIGHT *from the* BIBLE**
>
> *"When we were overwhelmed by sins, you forgave [made atonement for] our transgressions."*
>
> PSALM 65:3

Paid in full with one glass of milk

One dime left

One day, a poor boy who was selling goods from door to door to pay his way through school, found he had only one thin dime left, and he was hungry. He decided he would ask for a meal at the next house. However, he lost his nerve when a lovely young woman opened the door.

Instead of a meal, he asked for a drink of water. She thought he looked hungry and so she brought him a large glass of milk. He drank it slowly, and then asked, "How much do I owe you?"

Nothing to pay

"You don't owe me anything," she replied. "Mother has taught us never to accept pay for a kindness."

He said, "Then I thank you from my heart."

As Howard Kelly left that house, he not only felt stronger physically, but his faith in God and humankind was strengthened also. He had been ready to give up and quit.

Critically ill

Years later, that young woman became critically ill. The local doctors were baffled. They finally sent her to the big city, where they called in specialists to study her rare disease.

Dr. Howard Kelly was called in for the consultation. When he heard the name of the town she came from, he went down the hall of the hospital to her room. Dressed in his doctor's gown, he went in to see her. He recognized her at once. He went back to the consultation room determined to do his best to save her life. From that day, he gave special attention to this case.

Paid in full

After a long struggle, the battle was won. Dr. Kelly requested from the business office to pass the final billing to him for approval. He looked at it, then wrote something on the edge, and the bill was sent to her room. She feared to open it, for she was sure it would take the rest of her life to pay for it all.

Finally she looked, and something caught her attention on the side of the bill. She read these words:

"PAID IN FULL WITH ONE GLASS OF MILK"

(Signed)
Dr. Howard Kelly."

The Shadow of Death

Holman Hunt

The Manchester City Art Gallery houses a painting of Christ by Holman Hunt. It shows Jesus standing inside his father's carpenter shop in Nazareth. He has momentarily put his saw down and is stripped down to a cloth around his waist. A weary Jesus stretches his arms above his head, casting a shadow onto the wall, a shadow in the shape of a person crucified.

A long narrow tool rack hanging on the wall intersects perfectly with his shadow to give the impression of the crossbeam of the cross.

Mary is startled

There is a woman in the foreground on the left hand side. She kneels among the woodchips, with her hands resting upon a chest that houses the gifts of the magi. It is Mary, startled by the cross-like shadow cast by her son.

LIGHT from the BIBLE

[Simeon . . . said to Mary,] "and a sword will pierce your own soul too."

LUKE 2:35

The shadow of the cross

In his painting Hunt depicts what the Gospels record for us with words. The shadow of the cross was cast over Christ's life from the beginning. His death lies at the heart of his story.

Devotion

Cyrus

It is said that Cyrus, the founder of the Persian Empire, once captured a prince and his family. When they came before him, the monarch asked the prisoner, "What will you give me if I release you?"

"The half of my wealth," was his reply.

"And if I release your children?"

"Everything I possess."

"And if I release your wife?"

"Your Majesty, I will give myself."

"Wasn't Cyrus handsome?"

Cyrus was so moved by the prince's devotion that he freed them all.

> **LIGHT from the BIBLE**
>
> *"Then he released Barabbas to them. But he had Jesus flogged, and handed him over to be crucified."*
>
> MATTHEW 27:26

As they returned home, the prince said to his wife, "Wasn't Cyrus a handsome man!" With a look of deep love for her husband, she said to him, "I didn't notice. I could only keep my eyes on you – the one who was willing to give himself for me."

Quotation to ponder

"If Jesus Christ be God and died for me, then no sacrifice can be too great for me to make for Him."

C. T. STUDD

The story behind the painting of the Last Supper

Living people

Leonardo Da Vinci, the renowned Italian artist, received a commission to paint the Last Supper. It took him seven years to complete his masterpiece. The figures representing the twelve Apostles and Christ himself were painted from living people. The life-model for the painting of the figure of Jesus was chosen first.

Innocence and beauty

When it was decided that Da Vinci would paint this great picture, hundreds and hundreds of young men were carefully viewed in an attempt to find a face and personality exhibiting innocence and beauty, free from any signs of dissipation caused by sin. Finally, after weeks of laborious search, a young nineteen-year-old man was selected as a model for the portrayal of Christ. For six months Da Vinci worked on the production of this leading character of his famous painting.

LIGHT *from the* BIBLE

"Those who look to him are radiant; their faces are never covered with shame."

PSALM 34:5

Judas Iscariot

During the next six years, Da Vinci continued his labors on this sublime work of art. One by one, suitable people were chosen to represent each of the eleven Apostles, with space being left for the painting of the figure representing Judas Iscariot as the final task of this masterpiece. This was the Apostle, you remember, who betrayed his Lord for thirty pieces of silver. For weeks, Da Vinci searched for a man with a hard, callous face, with a countenance marked by scars of avarice, deceit, hypocrisy, and crime, a face that would delineate a

Quotation to ponder

"What will move you?
Will pity? Here is distress never the like.
Will duty? Here is a person never the like.
Will fear? Here is wrath never the like.
Will remorse? Here are sins never the like.
Will kindness? Here is love never the like.
Will bounty? Here are benefits never the like.
Will all these?
Here they be all, all in the highest degree."

LANCELOT ANDREWES,
PREACHING ABOUT THE
PASSION OF JESUS

LIGHT *from* the BIBLE

"It is impossible for those who have once been enlightened, who have tasted the heavenly gift, who have shared in the Holy Spirit, who have tasted the goodness of the word of God and the powers of the coming age, if they fall away, to be brought back to repentance, because to their loss they are crucifying the Son of God all over again and subjecting him to public disgrace."

HEBREWS 6:4-6

character who would betray his best friend. After many discouraging experiences in searching for the type of person required to represent Judas, word came to Da Vinci that a man whose appearance fully met his requirements had been found in a dungeon in Rome, sentenced to die for a life of crime and murder.

Complete ruin

Da Vinci made the trip to Rome at once, and this man was brought out from his imprisonment in the dungeon and led out into the light of the sun. There Da Vinci saw before him a dark, swarthy man, his long, shaggy, and unkempt hair sprawled over his face, which betrayed a character of viciousness and complete ruin. At last the famous painter had found the person he wanted to represent the character of Judas in his painting.

By special permission from the king, this prisoner was carried to Milan where the picture was being painted. For months he sat before Da Vinci at appointed hours each day, as the gifted artist diligently continued his task of transmitting to his painting, this base character representing the traitor and betrayer of our Savior.

As he finished his last stroke, he turned to the guards and said, "I have finished. You may take the prisoner away."

"Don't you recognize me?"

As the guards were leading their prisoner away, he suddenly broke loose from their control and rushed up to Da Vinci, crying as he did so, "Da Vinci, look at me. Do you not know who I am?"

Da Vinci, with the trained eyes of a great character student, carefully scrutinized the man upon whose face he had constantly gazed for six months and replied, "No, I have never seen you in my life until you were brought before me out of the dungeon in Rome."

Then, lifting his eyes toward heaven, the prisoner said, "Oh God, have I fallen so low?" Then turning his face to the painter he cried, "Leonardo Da Vinci, look at me again, for I am the same man you painted just seven years ago as the figure of Christ."

Quotation to ponder

"If you are not fit to take Communion you are not fit to pray, and if you are not fit to pray you are not fit to live, and if you are not fit to live, you are not fit to die."

D. MARTYN LLOYD-JONES

The three trees

Hopes and dreams

Once there were three trees on a hill in the woods. They were discussing their hopes and dreams.

The first little tree looked at the stars and said, "I want to hold treasure. I want to be covered with gold and filled with precious stones. I will be the most beautiful treasure chest in the world!"

The second little tree looked out at the small stream trickling by on its way to the ocean. "I want to be traveling mighty waters and carrying powerful kings. I'll be the strongest ship in the world. Everyone will feel safe in me because of the strength of my hull."

The third little tree looked down into the valley below where busy men and women worked in the busy town. "I don't want to leave this hill at all. I want to grow so tall that when people look at me, they'll raise their eyes to heaven and think of God. I will be the tallest tree in the world."

First tree

After a few years of praying that their dreams would come true, a group of woodsmen came upon the trees.

When one came to the first tree he said, "This looks like a strong tree, I think I should be able to sell the wood to a carpenter," and he began cutting it down. The tree was happy, because he knew that the carpenter would make him into a treasure chest.

Quotation to ponder

"There is a legitimate place for blood, sweat, and tears; but it should have its roots in the call of God, not in the desire to get ahead. Life is more than a climb to the top of the heap."

RICHARD J. FOSTER

Second tree
At the second tree a woodsman said, "This looks like a strong tree, I should be able to sell it to the shipyard." The second tree was happy because he knew he was on his way to becoming a mighty ship.

Third tree
When the woodsmen came upon the third tree, the tree was frightened because he knew that if they cut him down his dreams would not come true. One of the woodsmen said, "I don't need anything special from my tree so I'll take this one," and he cut it down.

Dreams forgotten
When the first tree arrived at the carpenters, he was made into a feed box for animals. He was then placed in a barn and filled with hay. This was not at all what he had prayed for.

The second tree was cut and made into a small fishing boat. His dreams of being a mighty ship and carrying kings had come to an end.

The third tree was cut into large pieces and left alone in the dark.

The years went by, and the trees forgot about their dreams.

First tree

Then one day, a man and woman came to the barn. She gave birth and they placed the baby in the hay in the feed box that was made from the first tree. The man wished that he could have made a crib for

> ## LIGHT *from the* BIBLE
>
> *"As they led him away, they seized Simon from Cyrene, who was on his way in from the country, and put the cross on him and made him carry it behind Jesus."*
>
> LUKE 23:26

the baby, but this manger would have to do. The tree could feel the importance of this event and knew that it had held the greatest treasure of all time.

Second tree

Years later, a group of men got in the fishing boat made from the second tree. One of them was tired and went to sleep. While they were out on the water, a great storm arose and the tree didn't think it was strong enough to keep the men safe. The men woke the sleeping man, and he stood and said "Peace" and the storm stopped. At this time, the tree knew that it had carried the King of Kings in its boat.

Third tree

Finally, someone came and got the third tree. She flinched as she was carried through an angry jeering crowd. She shuddered when soldiers nailed a man's hands to her. She felt ugly, harsh, and cruel. But, on Sunday morning, when the sun rose and the earth trembled with joy beneath her, the third tree knew that God's love had changed everything. It had made the third tree strong. And every time people thought of the third tree, they would think of God. That was better than being the tallest tree in the world.

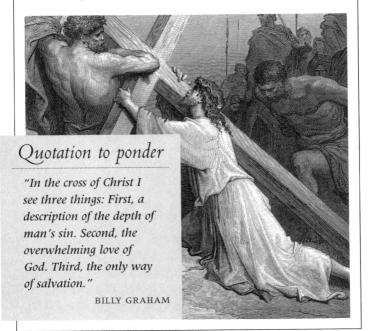

Quotation to ponder

"In the cross of Christ I see three things: First, a description of the depth of man's sin. Second, the overwhelming love of God. Third, the only way of salvation."

BILLY GRAHAM

— Part 2 —

TESTIMONIES TO
the Cross OF CHRIST

Mitsuo Fuchida

Pearl Harbor

Mitsuo Fuchida (1902–1976) was the General Commander of the Japanese air squadron that led the 360-plane attack on Pearl Harbor on 7 December 1941.

His spiritual pilgrimage led him through Shintoism, Buddhism, and Emperor Worship to Christianity.

Jacob DeShazer

On a journey to Tokyo in 1949 to meet General MacArthur, Fuchida was given a tract entitled, I Was A Prisoner of Japan. It told the story of Jacob DeShazer, an American who had been captured in special missions behind the Japanese lines. In prison he had been given a Bible, and through reading it had come to know Jesus Christ as his own Master and Lord. After the war he had returned to Japan as a missionary to the people whom he had once fought and hated.

> **LIGHT *from the* BIBLE**
>
> *"Two other men, both criminals, were also led out with him to be executed. When they came to the place called the Skull, there they crucified him, along with the criminals – one on his right, the other on his left. Jesus said, 'Father, forgive them, for they do not know what they are doing.' And they divided up his clothes by casting lots."*
>
> LUKE 23:32-34

The testimony of this tract had a profound effect on ex-Commander Fuchida and he began to read the Bible carefully himself.

Changed attitude

"The dynamic power of Christ which Jake DeShazer accepted into his life changed his entire attitude toward his captors. His hatred turned to love and concern, and he resolved that should his country win the war and he be liberated, he would someday return to Japan to introduce others to this life-changing book."

Peaceful motivation

"The peaceful motivation I had read about was exactly what I was seeking. Since the American had found it in the Bible, I decided to purchase one myself, despite my traditionally Buddhist heritage.

"In the ensuing weeks, I read this book eagerly. I came to the climactic drama – the Crucifixion. I read in Luke 23:34 the prayer of Jesus Christ at His death: 'Father, forgive them; for they know not what they do.'"

> ## Quotation to ponder
>
> *"I know the brutality and the cruelties of war better than many people. Now I want to work for peace. But how can mankind achieve a lasting peace? True peace of heart, mind, and soul can only come through Jesus Christ."*
>
> MITSUO FUCHIDA

"I was impressed that I was certainly one of those for whom He had prayed. The many men I had killed had been slaughtered in the name of patriotism, for I did not understand the love which Christ wishes to implant within every heart.

"I seemed to meet Jesus"

"Right at that moment, I seemed to meet Jesus for the first time. I understood the meaning of His death as a substitute for my wickedness, and so in prayer, I requested Him to forgive my sins and change me from a bitter, disillusioned ex-pilot into a well-balanced Christian with purpose in living.

April 14, 1950

"That date, April 14, 1950 – became the second 'day to remember' of my life. On that day, I became a new person. My complete view on life was changed by the intervention of the Christ I had always hated and ignored before. Soon other friends beyond my close family learned of my decision to be a follower of Christ, and they could hardly understand it.

An opportunist?

"Big headlines appeared in the papers: 'Pearl Harbor

> **LIGHT** *from the* **BIBLE**
>
> *"Then Peter came to Jesus and asked, 'Lord, how many times shall I forgive my brother when he sins against me? Up to seven times?' Jesus answered, 'I tell you, not seven times, but seventy-seven times.'"*
>
> MATTHEW 18:21-22

Hero Converts to Christianity.' Old war buddies came to visit me, trying to persuade me to discard 'this crazy idea.' Others accused me of being an opportunist, embracing Christianity only for how it might impress our American victors.

"But time has proven them wrong. As an evangelist, I have traveled across Japan and the Orient introducing others to the One Who changed my life."

Quotation to ponder

"He is the only One Who was powerful enough to change my life and inspire it with His thoughts. He was the only answer to Jake DeShazer's tormented life. He is the only answer for young people today."

MITSUO FUCHIDA

The only hope

"I believe with all my heart that those who will direct Japan – and all other nations – in the decades to come must not ignore the message of Jesus Christ.

"Youth must realize that He is the only hope for this troubled world."

A different kind of death-blow

"I would give anything to retract my actions at Pearl Harbor, but it is impossible. Instead, I now work at striking the death-blow to the basic hatred which infests the human heart and causes such tragedies. And that hatred cannot be uprooted without assistance from Jesus Christ."

Toyohiko Kagawa

Perhaps the most famous Asian Christian of the 20th century, Toyohiko Kagawa, a Japanese convert from a wealthy Buddhist family, spent many years living in the slums in various Japanese cities and dedicated himself to the improvement of social conditions for the poor.

"Make me like Christ"

Kagawa, at the age of 15, went to learn English from a Christian missionary in Japan, and the Gospel of Luke was

LIGHT from the BIBLE

". . . he went around doing good . . ."

ACTS 10:38

one of the texts he had to study. He read about the things Jesus did for people, and when he read how Jesus had been crucified he was amazed.

"Oh God," he prayed, "make me like Christ."

He was reluctant at first to seek baptism, because his uncle was paying for his education and Kagawa was worried about his uncle's reaction when he heard that his nephew had become a Christian. But his Christian teachers pointed out that this was cowardly, so he asked for baptism, and his uncle did not object – until Kagawa announced that he wanted to be ordained.

Kagawa's work in Japan

In the years that followed, Kagawa's prayers were answered, as he went about doing good, preaching to the poor, living for ten years with the slum derelicts in Kobe, Japan, and later establishing labor co-operatives, farmer unions, nurseries, and social welfare centers of all kinds.

When a newspaper ran a competition for the ten greatest names in Japanese history, Kagawa was at the top, and the only Christian mentioned. Yet in Japan, he was not always honored because he tended to by-pass the institutional churches.

Global ministry
He went on to live and work for the poorest people, to work for the state to allow trade unions, to preach Christ in Japan and abroad, to write 150 books and to denounce first his own country and then the USA and the Allies for their pursuit of war in the Second World War.

Denominations
When in English he spoke of "denominations," his listeners thought he said "damnations." He replied: "They are very much the same thing."

> ## Quotation to ponder
>
> *"There are two kinds of Christianity: success-Christianity and failure-Christianity. Jesus said, 'Unless I fail, my work will be useless.'"*
>
> TOYOHIKO KAGAWA

Socialist
He was, he said, not a Christian because he was interested in society's problems; he was, rather, a convinced socialist because he was a Christian.

Tokichi Ishii

Sub-human

One of the great conversion stories of modern times is the story of how the Japanese murderer Tokichi Ishii was converted by reading the New Testament when he was in prison. He was a man of the most savage cruelty, bestial and sub-human in the terrible crimes that he had committed.

Two Canadian women

He was converted by reading a Bible which two Canadian women left with him, when they could not

---

LIGHT *from the* BIBLE

"Two other men, both criminals, were also led out with him to be executed. When they came to the place called the Skull, there they crucified him, along with the criminals – one on his right, the other on his left. Jesus said, 'Father, forgive them, for they do not know what they are doing.' And they divided up his clothes by casting lots. The people stood watching, and the rulers even sneered at him. They said, 'He saved others; let him save himself if he is the Christ of God, the Chosen One.' The soldiers also came up and mocked him. They offered him wine vinegar and said, 'If you are the king of the Jews, save yourself.' There was a written notice above him, which read: THIS IS THE KING OF THE JEWS."

LUKE 23:32-38

---

get even a flicker of human response to anything they said to him.

He read it, and when he came to the prayer of Jesus: "Father, forgive them, they know not what they do," he said, "I stopped. I was stabbed to the heart as if pierced by a five inch nail." His sorrow for his sin was the sorrow of a broken heart. "Shall I call it the love of Christ? Shall I call it His compassion? I do not know what to call it. I only know that I believed and my hardness of heart was changed."

Later, when the condemned man went to the scaffold, he was no longer the hardened, surly brute he once had been, but a smiling radiant man. The murderer had been born again; Christ had brought Tokichi Ishii to life.

> ## Quotation to ponder
>
> *"Your heart is the altar of God. It is here that the fire of intense love must burn always. You are to feed it every day with the wood of the cross of Christ and the commemoration of his passion."*
>
> SAINT BONAVENTURE

— Part 3 —

MEL GIBSON'S
The Passion OF THE
CHRIST

Brutally attacked administrator

A healing movie

This is a healing movie in every way. My husband is a physician (internal medicine) and he went to see The Passion with an associate who is an administrator of a healthcare facility.

About six months ago our friend, the administrator, was brutally attacked by two unhappy employees. His jaw was broken and it has caused him considerable pain. He had to undergo oral surgery.

LIGHT *from* the BIBLE

"Forgive as the Lord forgave you."

COLOSSIANS 3:13

The two brothers

When he went in to view The Passion, he saw the two brothers there that had attacked him. They were on the opposite side of the auditorium. He said that he prayed for them that the film would be meaningful.

After the conclusion of *The Passion of the Christ*, the main perpetrator of the crime came over visibly shaken. He had been weeping. He looked up and asked our friend if he would forgive him for what he had done. Our friend confirmed that he had forgiven him.

My husband said that in knowing the facts of what

had happened and a little of the basics about the incident, he considered what he had witnessed an Act of God.

❖ Posted on *The Passion of the Christ* website

Quotation to ponder

"The Passion of Jesus is the greatest and most overwhelming work of God's love."

ST. PAUL OF THE CROSS

A gay man afflicted with AIDS

This is a true account of how a modern-day "leper" – a gay man afflicted with AIDS – was brought to the loving and merciful heart of our Lord Jesus as a result of seeing Mel Gibson's The Passion of the Christ. I am able to attest to the facts of the case because I was there and witnessed it.

Sean's story

I'm sharing Sean's story with his permission, as a testament to the transformational power of this miraculous film. I first met Sean over a decade ago, through a girl whom I was dating at the time. She was a hairdresser at an upscale salon, and he was one of her co-workers. They were good friends, and we occasionally ran into him on social outings. He was funny and charming, and a very kind person.

> **LIGHT *from the* BIBLE**
>
> *"A man with leprosy came and knelt before him and said, 'Lord, if you are willing, you can make me clean.' Jesus reached out his hand and touched the man. 'I am willing,' he said. 'Be clean!' Immediately he was cured of his leprosy."*
>
> MATTHEW 8:2-3

He was gay

And he was also gay. This was a problem for Sean. He had been raised in a strict, fundamentalist environment in which homosexuality was viewed as an E-pass straight to hell.

He believed in God, and was baptized, and had been "saved" as a boy, yet he also knew that he was gay, from as far back as he could remember. This conflict caused great

> *Quotation to ponder*
>
> "*Sin and disease are evil, definite evil, not imperfect good; they do not call for improvement, they call for destruction.*"
>
> G. STUDDERT KENNEDY

emotional suffering for him. He believed that because he was homosexual, whether he acted on it or not, he would be forever cut off from the presence of God.

In spite of his yearning for God, Sean believed there was no room at Christ's table for an abomination such as him, so he resigned himself to God's unsparing wrath and the inevitable afterlife in the fiery pits of eternal damnation.

He contracted AIDS

With that to look forward to, he must've decided at some point to get what little joy he could out of his short time on this earth, so he allowed himself to fall in love. And he sinned.

I, too, was a great sinner at that time. But being heterosexual, my sins were far less potentially lethal than those of Sean's. Some time later, I learned that he had contracted AIDS.

Lost contact

I ran into Sean from time to time over the following years, and noticed how gaunt he had become, and learned that he could no longer work because of his disability, and the powerful drug cocktails, etc.

Months and years passed, and I had no idea what had happened to him. Nor, to my everlasting shame, did I care enough to go out of my way to find out.

LIGHT *from the* BIBLE

"Jesus continued: 'There was a man who had two sons. The younger one said to his father, 'Father, give me my share of the estate.' So he divided his property between them. Not long after that, the younger son got together all he had, set off for a distant country and there squandered his wealth in wild living.'"

LUKE 15:11-13

Fast forward to Good Friday last

I had been planning to go to church that evening, when an opportunity presented itself: I ran into Sean. I invited him to go to church with me later that evening, but he wasn't comfortable with the idea. I understood, so I didn't press the issue.

Instead, I asked him if he'd seen *The Passion of the Christ*. He hadn't seen it yet, but to my astonishment, he said that he very much wanted to. The only problem was that he didn't have a car, and he couldn't afford the price of a ticket, since he was on disability, with a very restricted income.

So, instead of going to church that night, I took Sean to the movies. *The Passion of the Christ*, of course. It would be my sixth time seeing it in a theater – and certainly not the last, as I intend to see it again several more times. (I used to think those Star Wars "geeks" were a little nutty for going to see the same film over and over again: I guess I've become an unashamed "geek" for Christ.)

Overwhelming impact

He'd heard all about the movie – about how intense it was, and about how it was touching people's lives. But just like me the first time I saw it, nothing he'd heard about the film prepared him for its overwhelming impact.

He was cheery and talkative during the previews, TV promos, and public service announcements. But once

> ## Quotation to ponder
>
> *"The sins of the flesh are bad, but they are the least bad of all sins. All the worst pleasures are purely spiritual: the pleasure of putting other people in the wrong, of bossing and patronizing and spoiling sport and backbiting; the pleasures of power; of hatred."*
>
> C. S. LEWIS

the film started – without any opening credits, plunging us straight into the moonlit garden of Gethsemane during Christ's dark night of the soul – he became very quiet.

Already, the film was beginning to work its quiet miracle.

The scourging

Then came the scene of Pilate's "chastisement." The scourging. The theater, which was packed that Good Friday night, was filled with the muffled sounds of stifled weeping. (Even though I'd seen the film five times before, my own eyes were hardly dry.) As I glanced over at Sean I saw that his head was bowed. He was silently weeping, the tears dropping onto the tightly clenched hands at his waist. He was praying!

> ### LIGHT *from the* BIBLE
>
> *"Wanting to satisfy the crowd, Pilate released Barabbas to them. He had Jesus flogged, and handed him over to be crucified. The soldiers led Jesus away into the palace (that is, the Praetorium) and called together the whole company of soldiers. They put a purple robe on him, then twisted together a crown of thorns and set it on him. And they began to call out to him, 'Hail, king of the Jews!'"*
>
> MARK 15:15-18

Almost too much to bear

The film was almost too much for him to bear. The scene where Jesus falls under the Cross and Mary comes to him – and Jesus says, "See, Mother, how I make all things new!" especially effected him.

Sean was so overcome with emotion that he bolted out of his chair and darted from the theater for fear of crying out. I started after him, but he frantically waved me back. He returned a few minutes later, having composed himself.

The crucifixion
And then, of course, came the crucifixion, which was wrenching beyond words.

Quotation to ponder

[As we watched The Passion of the Christ,*] "I heard a weeping voice say, 'I'm sorry, Lord. Forgive me, Lord.' Our cries became part of the soundtrack."*

CHONDA PIERCE

LIGHT *from the* BIBLE

"A certain man from Cyrene, Simon, the father of Alexander and Rufus, was passing by on his way in from the country, and they forced him to carry the cross. They brought Jesus to the place called Golgotha (which means The Place of the Skull). Then they offered him wine mixed with myrrh, but he did not take it. And they crucified him. Dividing up his clothes, they cast lots to see what each would get. It was the third hour when they crucified him."

MARK 15:21-25

After the film

After the film, as the end titles scrolled up the screen, he turned to me and said through his tears, "That wasn't just a movie."

"I know," I replied, my own eyes still moist.

"It brought me to a place I'd never been before, to a place I never imagined I'd go. It brought me to Christ."

After seeing *The Passion of the Christ*, Sean had a deep conversion of heart, just as I did. Like me, he finally grasped the depth of Christ's love for us in spite of our sins and failings, and is now a devout Christian. He's been attending a local church on an almost daily basis in order to strengthen his new-found faith.

This I attest to, having seen for myself.
A miraculous film. There's no other word for it. It worked a miracle in my life, and here again it works yet another one.

Instruments of divine intervention

There is not an atom of doubt – none – that Mel Gibson and Jim Caviezel, and everybody involved in the creation of this extraordinary film were truly the instruments of divine intervention in our hurting world. God bless them, every one. And God bless all of you.

love,

    Jack

❖ Posted on *The Passion of the Christ* website

Quotation to ponder

"No film in my lifetime has the potential of impacting more people with the world's greatest story than The Passion."

TIM LAHAYE

A cold breeze across our faces

I took my three teenage girls, and my friend Joe and his wife, to see The Passion of the Christ. *We survived the movie but we will carry scars for the rest of our lives.*

Like eye-witnesses

It was as if we were witnesses to the beating, the desecration of the flesh, the inhuman struggle to the cross, and the shedding of the blood of the Lamb of God.

The tears started flowing when the scourging started. They continued even after the movie was over. The front of my shirt was soaked. I don't think there was a dry eye in the house.

One lady left balling her eyes out when the beating started and that was the easy part of the movie. She never returned. I wanted to just give her a shoulder to cry on as she hurried up the aisle.

> **LIGHT *from the* BIBLE**
>
> *"Surely he took up our infirmities and carried our sorrows, yet we considered him stricken by God, smitten by him, and afflicted. But he was pierced for our transgressions, he was crushed for our iniquities; the punishment that brought us peace was upon him, and by his wounds we are healed."*
>
> ISAIAH 53:4-5

The wind began to blow

This has to be the most graphical portrayal of suffering ever put to film. The stripes were more than one can bear. If one did not know the story one would think Jesus would not make it to the cross alive. As bad as the cross must have been, it was a relief from the pain and suffering that came before it.

When Jesus took his final breath the wind began to blow, not just on the mountain but through the theater we all felt a cold breeze across our faces.

Overflowing with emotion

This is not a movie for young kids or weak hearts. I may never be able to watch it again. It is that powerful. It is overflowing with emotion that grabs you by the heart and refuses to let go. I could not speak, I could only stand by and watch. All the while, I wanted so much to just stop the pain and suffering. We all did.

Mel your message is being seen and understood – around the world. You sought the truth, found it, and documented it for all of mankind.

❖ Posted on *The Passion of the Christ* website

Quotation to ponder

"Anyone who has not been troubled by the scandal of Christ's suffering and his complete humiliation is ignorant of the meaning of belief in him."

JOHANN HEINRICH ARNOLD

Billy Graham and The Passion of the Christ

A true evangelist

I heard of a traditional Catholic who said that he considered Billy Graham to be a heretic and would not listen to anything he had to say. I can't help but find that statement to be a bit scary (for the person who said it).

> **LIGHT *from* the BIBLE**
>
> *"For I resolved to know nothing while I was with you except Jesus Christ and him crucified."*
>
> 1 CORINTHIANS 2:2

Billy Graham became a Christian in 1934. He is now 85 years old and has preached to more people than anyone in history. A true evangelist, he has preached the Gospel of Jesus Christ to 210,000,000 people in 185 different countries. (That's just so far, those numbers are ever growing.) He has known and/or been the spiritual advisor to every American president since Harry Truman in 1945.

As a child of seven

While vacationing at my grandparents' home on Prince Edward Island, Canada, I, a Roman Catholic child of seven, said the sinners' prayer and gave my life to Jesus Christ after watching a Billy Graham crusade on a little b/w television. I would say that youth and the lack of teaching caused me to forget that moment for a period of time, but God didn't forget and I was reminded years later when I was born again.

Mel Gibson, Jim Caviezel, and Billy Graham
Interestingly, and this is how it all relates to *The Passion of the Christ*, Mel Gibson and Jim Caviezel made two trips to Billy Graham's home in North Carolina to visit with him and bring him The Passion to view. They met with him once before the viewing and once after.

> *Quotation to ponder*
>
> "*There is no more urgent and critical question in life than that of your personal relationship with God and your eternal salvation.*"
>
> BILLY GRAHAM

Afterwards Mel Gibson, a traditional Catholic, said to Jim, "Well, we got to meet Billy Graham. I've always wanted to meet him."

Jim Caviezel's statements
The following are statements Jim Caviezel made after his meeting with Billy Graham. (Looks like Jim and I have something in common.)

"I got to be with him for three hours and he is a wonderful man. When we met, I told him, 'I believe you carry the Holy Spirit with you; I believe you are a holy man.'"

"What moved me the most about him was that he gets out of the way and allows God to come through. It's so easy to give the truth with a bit of your own spin on it. He doesn't. He speaks from his heart. He prays from the heart, and we're forever grateful to him.

"When I heard him speak [on television] years ago, it was in the middle of the night, and I couldn't deny – there was something inside me that said, 'This is the truth.' I recognized truth from the start, and I had to answer it. It doesn't matter if this person hits you or your father did this to you or whatever, the truth still exists out there. Something I couldn't quite put into words at fifteen years old. It gave me a hope."

> **LIGHT** *from the* **BIBLE**
>
> *". . . but we preach Christ crucified: a stumbling block to Jews and foolishness to Gentiles."*
>
> 1 CORINTHIANS 1:23

The same Holy Spirit

Sounds to me like Jim responded to the same truth that I and millions of others have responded to after hearing Billy Graham preach the Gospel. It's because the Holy Spirit is present and speaking to the hearts of the millions who have given their lives to Jesus through this man's ministry. I'm glad to know that Mel and Jim put so much stock in Billy Graham's opinion and that they were so excited to meet him and get his reactions to the film.

Billy Graham's endorsement

Billy Graham gave *The Passion of the Christ* his heartfelt endorsement and said many amazing things about this incredible inspired work.

"No one who views this film's compelling imagery will ever be the same."

❖ Posted on *The Passion of the Christ* website

Quotation to ponder

"I have often wondered what it must have been like to be a bystander during those last hours before Jesus' death. After watching **The Passion of the Christ**, I feel as if I have actually been there."

"I was moved to tears. I doubt if there has ever been a more graphic and moving presentation of Jesus' death and resurrection – which Christians believe are the most important events in human history."

"The film is faithful to the Bible's teaching that we are all responsible for Jesus' death, because we have all sinned. It is our sins that caused His death, not any particular group."

BILLY GRAHAM

Caroline

Drained

Like you and many others here, I also went to see *The Passion of the Christ* yesterday, with my teenaged daughter. For the remainder of the day, images kept flashing across my mind. I felt physically and emotionally drained, my eyes swollen from crying.

Varying reactions

To all the clerics in the Catholic and Greek Orthodox Church who dread an anti-Semitic reaction, I asked my daughter if the movie had altered her view of the Jews. It did not. I might contrast their reaction to that of the Evangelical ministers. They have booked entire theaters and bused in their congregations. Where are the Catholic prelates? Why aren't they encouraging their flocks to see a living Stations of the Cross? Because they are as blind as the Chief Priests and other members of the Sanhedrin! They cower in the shadow of the crucifix, assuming they haven't yet replaced it with one of those Risen Christ statues, like my parish.

> **LIGHT *from* the BIBLE**
>
> "... Jesus, who was crucified."
>
> MATTHEW 28:5

Peter's denial

I was very moved by the scene where Peter, realizing that he has denied Christ three times, slumps down against the side of the pillar, eyes glazed over, flashback to the words Christ spoke to him, mouth open, body trembling.

In him I saw all of us who have sinned, confessed, promised never to sin again and caved in through weakness. It was so powerful!

> ## Quotation to ponder
>
> *"The death of Jesus Christ holds the secret of the mind of God."*
>
> OSWALD CHAMBERS

Mary

I have had a difficult time all of my life relating to Mary. Thank you Mel Gibson and Maia Morgenstern for bringing Mary to life! Watching her mop up the blood in the courtyard, the expression on her face was one that only a mother could understand. It was a look of steady determination as she gathered the Precious Blood of her Son. When she kissed the toes on his foot as he hung from the cross, I recalled the Good Friday service when we venerate the cross. I plan to see the movie again on Good Friday.

Francis of Assisi

Lastly, it was St. Francis of Assisi who gave us the nativity to venerate at Christmas. And now it is (St.) Mel who has given us The Passion of the Cross to commemorate Good Friday and Easter.

Thank you, Mr. Gibson! Pax et Bonum.

❖ Posted on *The Passion of the Christ* website

Crime confessions

Far from sparking off any outbreaks of violence, as critics of Mel Gibson's film, The Passion of the Christ, had suggested, it has prompted a number of criminals to confess to crimes they committed.

Mesa, Arizona

In Mesa, Arizona, it has been reported that Turner Lee Bingham told the police, who were at the scene of a burglary, that he had committed it. He said he had taken $80 from the register. He also owned up to five other break-ins.

A Mesa police detective, Ruben Quesada, is reported to have said: "He had made some mention that after watching the Mel Gibson movie that gave him his motive for turning himself in."

The owner of the shop, Tobias Bright, is quoted as saying to the police, "If you're going to be burglarized, I don't think it could turn out any better."

Norway

"The trigger that made him go to police and confess was that movie,"

> **LIGHT *from the* BIBLE**
>
> *"He who has been stealing must steal no longer, but must work, doing something useful with his own hands, that he may have something to share with those in need."*
>
> EPHESIANS 4:28

his lawyer, Fridtjof Feydt, told Reuters on Monday. In Norway, a neo-Nazi, Johnny Olsen, 41, confessed that he had been responsible for some unexplained bombings against anarchist squatters in Oslo in 1994 and 1995.

Olsen is reported to have said that he had to confess to this crime "after watching Gibson's depiction of the suffering and death of Jesus Christ."

Confession of murder

A man who lives near Houston has been moved by his experience viewing The Passion. He has confessed to killing his girlfriend, when her death had previously been believed to be suicide. This man said he confessed to this because he was seeking "redemption."

> ## Quotation to ponder
>
> *"Repentance ranges from regretting obvious sins like murder, adultery, abuse, swearing, and stealing to the realization that not loving (loving your brother as yourself) is a murder, and that an evil look is adultery and the love of praise is stealing God's glory."*
>
> JOHN CHRYSOSTOM

Florida

A man who robbed a bank two years ago in Florida turned himself in to police as a result of watching Gibson's film.

I am sixteen years old

LIGHT from the BIBLE

"I have been crucified with Christ and I no longer live, but Christ lives in me. The life I live in the body, I live by faith in the Son of God, who loved me and gave himself for me."

GALATIANS 2:20

Genius

I am 16 years old and I have already seen The Passion of the Christ three times. That movie is genius. It touched my heart in so many ways and helped me to understand what our Lord went through for us. I think that everyone who has seen that movie is extremely blessed to have seen such an awesome film. Just thinking about it makes me sad and emotional but the movie had plenty of love messages from Jesus Christ to his people who he laid his life down for. So even though he suffered so much, he is appreciated and loved.

Many miracles

Today at church, my pastor had a good message. He said that as many times as we may want to see Jesus and praise him for being the Son of God, it is better that we stay down here on Earth so that he can watch over all of us and live through all of us in the form of the Holy Spirit until we meet him on that final day. But even if I don't see God, I can feel him with me every day and everywhere. It is amazing how many miracles *The Passion of the Christ* has created.

Increased understanding

I loved God before seeing the movie but I never fully understood Jesus' sacrifice and now that I have seen the movie, I understand it completely and he is forever in my heart.

Thanks to Mel Gibson and everyone who made that film possible, people are being brought to a better side of life, the life of our Lord. I will live for him and praise him forever. I just hope that many will appreciate *The Passion of the Christ* and be converted to him.

God Bless all.

❖ Posted on *The Passion of the Christ* website

Hymn to ponder

There is a green hill far away,
Outside a city wall,
Where the dear Lord was crucified,
Who died to save us all.

REFRAIN
O dearly, dearly, has He loved,
And we must love Him, too,
And trust in His redeeming blood,
And try His works to do.

CECIL F. ALEXANDER

I am so sorry, Jesus

Every Friday

I went to see TPOTC for my fifth time last Saturday. One viewing for each of my Lord's wounds (the big ones). Now the film's gone from our cinemas, but I'll buy the DVD as soon as it's available and then I'll watch it every Friday. The idea of watching it as many times as there are scars on my Precious One's body appeals to me.

LIGHT from the BIBLE

"One of the criminals who hung there hurled insults at him: 'Aren't you the Christ? Save yourself and us!' But the other criminal rebuked him. 'Don't you fear God,' he said, 'since you are under the same sentence? We are punished justly, for we are getting what our deeds deserve. But this man has done nothing wrong.' Then he said, 'Jesus, remember me when you come into your kingdom.'"

LUKE 23:39-42

A spiritual experience

For me too, this isn't just a film, but an intense spiritual experience. Oh, how I love Jesus! And it makes me so sad to think that it hasn't always been like this. I have sinned a lot and didn't realize that my life was paid for in blood – His Blood! And sometimes I was aware that my sinning hurt Him, but didn't care enough to stop. And I always made up some excuse for my behavior... I AM SO SORRY, JESUS!!! I never want to hurt You again!

Fifth viewing

My fifth viewing was all about my relationship with Jesus. I saw how much I have in common with Judas, Peter, Simon of Cyrene, Magdalene, Veronica, and the criminal who asked the Lord to think of him. I realized how much I have hurt Him, denied Him, betrayed Him, abused Him, and told Him to carry His cross alone, as I couldn't be bothered to help. While all the time it was MY cross He was carrying!!!

I felt so ashamed, so heartbroken, and yet so filled with love and gratitude!

> ## Quotation to ponder
>
> *"Only the way of the cross leads home."*
>
> BILLY GRAHAM

I was swept away

I love the criminal's words on the cross and I was swept away with the look Jesus gave him in return. Did you see that Jesus looked at him with both His eyes open?! I was so touched by this scene!

"Lord, I have sinned, and my punishment is justified. You could rightfully condemn me. Yet I ask You to think of me when You come into Your Kingdom."

Wow! This really sums up my whole life!

❖ Posted on *The Passion of the Christ* website

A new spin on my life

I saw The Passion just yesterday and for the first time, I saw an honest (as honest as it can get) portrayal of the last twelve hours of His life.

It certainly puts a new spin on my life. When I am upset about things not going the way I want it to, I usually get really upset. This movie reminds me that there is a greater power at work in all of our lives – He who made the ultimate sacrifice for all of us.

LIGHT from the BIBLE

"He was assigned a grave with the wicked, and with the rich in his death, though he had done no violence, nor was any deceit in his mouth."

ISAIAH 53:9

Quotation to ponder

"The most intense and moving motion picture I have ever seen. I have no doubt that many lives will be changed as a result of seeing it."

DR. JAMES KENNEY

Thanks

Thank you Mr. Gibson for having the guts, the passion, and absolute faith in Him to make this movie. May His Spirit continue to move you as it resulted in something so beautiful that has moved me. Thanks

❖ Posted on *The Passion of the Christ* website

James Caviezel mistaken for Jesus

Mexico

James Caviezel has been swamped with requests to perform miracles. Hundreds of Mexican fans believed he really was Jesus Christ.

LIGHT *from* the BIBLE

"For he had healed many, so that those with diseases were pushing forward to touch him."

MARK 3:10

The 35-year-old actor, who played Jesus in Mel Gibson's *The Passion of the Christ*, was on a one-week tour of the east Mexican state of Veracruz.

According to Mexican newspaper Reforma, dozens of residents from villages throughout the state, one of the poorest in the country, asked Caviezel to heal the sick and perform other miracles as he passed through.

Moved

The actor said: "The belief of these people really moved me. It was a shock for me to see how they came up to me to ask for my help. I had to explain to them that I was only an actor, and wasn't really the Son of God."

Quotation to ponder

'He healed the broken in heart, and bindeth up their wounds'

PSALM 147:3

My eyes are opened to the truth

Grandmother's gift

My girlfriend told me recently that my life was leading up to being in the faith of Jesus Christ. I had always had this faith that Jesus watched over me, but I did nothing to acknowledge his love for me.

My grandmother blessed me with the gift of giving my girlfriend and me tickets to The Passion of the Christ. My God, how my life was changed!

Endless tears

I don't know when I started crying (I faintly remember just before the flogging sequence), but the tears did not end. Holding myself half the film and my beloved girlfriend the other half, I nearly split in two from crying so hard.

Finally, the sequence of Christ's crucifixion, I lost it. Holding my head in my hands, praying endless for forgiveness, I was changed. I felt Christ comforting me, warming my heart. The film ended and the credits began to roll and the audience around me struggled to pull themselves out of their seats. But I sat there, flashing memories of the film back in my head and continuing to cry.

Two parts
It was a wonderful moment in my life. I saw my existence as divided into two parts: before discovering my Savior Jesus Christ and after discovering my Savior.

In the few months since, I have walked back into a church with a purpose for my life: to bring Jesus Christ into every person's heart that I walk by. To tell them the Truth.

And to Mel Gibson, thank you for allowing me to rediscover the Truth.

❖ Posted on *The Passion of the Christ* website

Quotation to ponder

"This Jesus of Nazareth, without money and arms, conquered more millions than Alexander, Caesar, Mohammed, and Napoleon; without science and learning, He shed more light on things human and divine than all philosophers and scholars combined; without the eloquence of schools, He spoke such words of life as were never spoken before or since and produced effects which lie beyond the reach of orator or poet; without writing a single line, He set more pens in motion, and furnished themes for more sermons, orations, discussions, learned volumes, works of art, and songs of praise, than the whole army of great men of ancient and modern times."

PHILIP SCHAFF

The Passion and my sobriety

Changed life

My life has been so changed it's amazing. I'm not even sure I know the words to explain it all.

First some background: I was brought up in the Episcopal Church and still go to the same church

LIGHT from the BIBLE

"Therefore, if anyone is in Christ, he is a new creation; the old has gone, the new has come!"

2 CORINTHIANS 5:17

with my family. I've never been what you would call a Bible-thumper, but I've always gotten some serenity from my church activities. I don't go to church every Sunday, but more like once or twice a month. The traditions and familiarity are what have brought me peace.

A recovering alcoholic

I've been in recovery for nine months now. I attend [Alcoholic Anonymous] meetings regularly, four to five times a week, have a fantastic sponsor and have grown spiritually in ways I never knew possible. The one thing that has been bothering me a bit though is trying to reconcile my religious view of God and my program view of God. I've learned I'm not unique in this.

For me, I absolutely HAD to be rigorously honest with myself regarding my beliefs or else I knew I would drink again. What I found was that my program spirituality was more comfortable and user-friendly to me than my religion. I seemed unable to reconcile these two.

As uncomfortable and weird as this has been, the God of my understanding has been, and still is, OK with it (whew).

A tangible view of God
Last week I saw *The Passion of the Christ* and it affected me in profound and far-reaching ways. While I didn't think I walked out of the movie theater Born Again,

Quotation to ponder

"1. We admitted we were powerless over alcohol –
that our lives had become unmanageable.

2. Came to believe that a Power greater than
ourselves could restore us to sanity.

3. Made a decision to turn our will and our lives
over to the care of God as we understood Him.

4. Made a searching and fearless moral inventory of
ourselves.

5. Admitted to God, to ourselves and to another
human being the exact nature of our wrongs."

THE TWELVE STEPS OF ALCOHOLICS ANONYMOUS:
STEPS 1-5

I did come out of there with a tangible view of God.
A human form of God, if you will. I have to say that
I really understood this for the first time in my life.

Visual context

When I was a teenager (though I must confess, I still do
this from time to time), when I saw a video of some song
that I had heard previously only on the radio, somehow
the visualization had impact. It added context to my
understanding of it. That's what I felt like walking out
of the movie theater; like I had some visual context that
I needed to have in order to begin to better understand
the God in my life. For the first time since grade school,
I pulled out my Bible this week and I've been reading about Jesus.

> **LIGHT** *from*
> *the* **BIBLE**
>
> *"For the Son of Man
> came to seek and to save
> what was lost."*
> LUKE 19:10

"Thy will be done"

This week I've been able
to get out of my own way
a little more than I've
been able to in the past; to be a better vehicle for
whatever it is that God has planned for me.

"Thy will, not mine, be done." I have said this over
and over to myself when I find myself trying to control
outcomes or feeling disappointed in the people, places,
and things in my life right now.

Somehow this movie has helped me to improve my
conscious contact with God as I understand him.

Quotation to ponder

"6. Were entirely ready to have God remove all these defects of character.

7. Humbly asked Him to remove our shortcomings.

8. Made a list of all persons we had harmed, and became willing to make amends to them all.

9. Made direct amends to such people wherever possible, except when to do so would injure them or others."

THE TWELVE STEPS OF ALCOHOLICS ANONYMOUS:
STEPS 6-9

The lonely and the lost

Someone told me this week "Jesus came for the lost, the lonely, and the hurting. We are the ones who need Him most."

I've been reading so much about this since I dusted off my Bible last week. Some of the things that have been meaningful to me about this: the lady with the lost coin, how the shepherd is so full of joy having found a lost lamb, the prodigal son story.

After reading these I feel so grateful to have Jesus back into my life. I'm starting to understand that it is OK not to be perfect to be accepted by God. I can't explain how powerful this is for me right now. I feel so full of relief and humbled that as I type this I sit here crying.

It's OK to ask for help

It seems it's knowledge that has always been there, but I didn't believe it. Because I felt so lost and not always sure I have complete faith, so I thought it would be better if I just stayed away. Now I'm starting to understand that's what Jesus came here to do and that it is OK to need him and OK to ask for his help.

Asking for God's guidance

I don't have to be perfect in order to ask for help. I'm not sure why in my mind this has always been so twisted but I have a hard time asking for help from anyone. I just never thought of it in relation to

> **LIGHT** *from the* **BIBLE**
>
> *". . . whoever comes to me I will never drive away."*
>
> JOHN 6:37

God. Since my new awakening (I don't really know what else to call it!) it is He to whom I have been turning first. It is difficult since I'm so self-centered, but this week I've really been learning and practicing by asking God's guidance through Jesus.

Glad to be an alcoholic!

Today I am so grateful to be an alcoholic. I've heard this said so much in meetings, but never really understood it until now. For me, the biggest reason I'm grateful is because AA has made religion more palatable for me. It has given me a way to lay my enormous ego down and invite the Lord back into my life.

Born again?

Earlier I wrote something like I didn't walk out of the movie Born Again. I'm not sure what else I could possibly call it though admittedly I'm not sure I know what it really means, at least as an official term. Today, somewhere in the Bible I read about being reborn and that truly is how I have felt since seeing The Passion.

Now that I've found my way back again, I pray to stay humble and understanding and continue to seek God's will for me.

Guess I found a few words after all.

❖ Posted on *The Passion of the Christ* website

Quotation to ponder

"10. *Continued to take personal inventory and when we were wrong promptly admitted it.*

11. *Sought through prayer and meditation to improve our conscious contact with God, as we understood Him, praying only for knowledge of His will for us and the power to carry that out.*

12. *Having had a spiritual awakening as the result of these steps, we tried to carry this message to alcoholics, and to practice these principles in all our affairs.*"

THE TWELVE STEPS OF ALCOHOLICS ANONYMOUS:
STEPS 10-12

The willingness of the Lord

Heart to heart

I can say with certainty that this is one of the best movies ever made. I have no doubt in my mind that what Mel Gibson has shown in this movie is as true and accurate as any man of God can get. I do believe that it came from God's heart to Mel's heart. We have candy-coated so long what it meant for Christ to be crucified, seeing in our minds an image of Christ on the cross and not understanding what really happened that day.

> **LIGHT from the BIBLE**
>
> "And he said, 'The Son of Man must suffer many things and be rejected by the elders, chief priests and teachers of the law, and he must be killed and on the third day be raised to life.'"
>
> LUKE 9:22

Our Lord's willingness

The thing that stands out most in my mind about this movie is the WILLINGNESS of the Lord to go through each and every step of the crucifixion, from the time when He was praying in the garden to fulfill God's plan until the time when He took His last breath on earth while on the cross.

The image I keep seeing over and over in my mind is when He could no longer stand up and He was lying on the ground there beside His cross, He dragged His body over to the cross, willingly trying to place Himself on the cross! There is no doubt in my mind that this just has to be what really happened. He knew that He had to be there and He willingly tried to put Himself there.

Thank you, Lord
Thank you, Lord, for dying for my sins for I surely don't deserve it.

Thank you for willingly being accused when there was no crime.

Thank you for willingly taking the beatings for me, and willingly dying for me.

Thank you to Mel Gibson and the actors and producers of this movie for taking a stand and not being afraid to tell the truth. I am so grateful that my Lord lives forever and I will be with Him in paradise someday.

❖ Posted on *The Passion of the Christ* website

Quotation to ponder

"Your heart is the altar of God. It is here that the fire of intense love must burn always. You are to feed it every day with the wood of the cross of Christ and the commemoration of his passion."

BONAVENTURE

This is what love is

An execution

I have witnessed an execution – not in real life, but startlingly realistic, in any case. Having had the privilege of experiencing Mel Gibson's highly controversial movie The Passion of the Christ *three times, I must say that everything I'd heard, read, and seen prior to my first viewing, held true. Everything, that is, except the unfair accusations of racial injustice. I found none of that. In keeping with the Scriptures, the movie stays on point, save some subtle embellishment by rights of artistic license from its producer/director.*

> ### LIGHT *from the* BIBLE
>
> **"When Jesus had finished saying all these things, he said to his disciples, 'As you know, the Passover is two days away – and the Son of Man will be handed over to be crucified.' Then the chief priests and the elders of the people assembled in the palace of the high priest, whose name was Caiaphas, and they plotted to arrest Jesus in some sly way and kill him."**
>
> MATTHEW 26:1-4

Final assessment

Incredibly well done!

In the darkened theater, audible sobs and whispered prayers could be heard, as the unrelenting torture of our precious Lord and Savior unfolded onscreen and made its way to the eyes, ears, and hearts of the riveted audience.

My sin

So what was I thinking throughout those two hours? Digesting the brutality in spurts, dissolved in tears – reeling from the intense emotion, and conscious the whole while that it is MY sin that is responsible for this horrible event that fairly defies description, I offered up private, silent contrition.

Spiritual to ponder

Were you there when they crucified my Lord?

Were you there when they crucified my Lord?

Oh! Sometimes it causes me to tremble, tremble, tremble.

Were you there when they crucified my Lord?

AFRICAN-AMERICAN
SPIRITUAL

Motherhood transcended

Watching "Mary" and realizing that her heart shattered with each stroke of the whip, each stumble, each fall, a kindred bond of motherhood transcended.

In shocked disbelief, and without protest, she followed her Son, "flesh of my flesh; heart of my heart" every step along His torturous journey, submitting fully to His Father's will, and thereby fulfilling the prophecy of Scripture.

An endearing scene

By now, the following account depicts a very familiar scene to those who've viewed the movie. But to those reading this, who might not have yet, may I offer this

LIGHT *from the* BIBLE

"Greater love hath no man than this, that a man lay down his life for his friends."

JOHN 15:13 KJV

tender enticement: Although most of this movie was disturbingly graphic in nature, one part was particularly gentle and endeared itself to me. It is a flashback that shows a young adult Jesus at home with his mother.

She is calling him in to eat, but he is admiring a table he's just built. Unable to get his attention, she walks outside and, observing the height of the finished product, she comments that she hopes whoever uses it intends to eat standing up. Jesus laughs and explains that he plans to build chairs to fit, then proceeds to demonstrate, assuming a sitting position at the table. She follows suit, then predicts that this idea will never catch on; both are amused.

Heading indoors Mary cautions Yeshuah (in Aramaic) to remove his dirty carpenter's apron before going into the house. "And wash your hands," she prompts, pouring water over his fingers from a pitcher she's carrying. After allowing the water to rinse over his hands, Jesus playfully splashes droplets in his mom's face, then embraces her and gives her a tender kiss on the cheek before going inside.

In stark contrast, the scene was lighthearted and showed us the humanness of Christ.

> ## Spiritual to ponder
>
> *Were you there when they nailed Him to the tree?*
> *Were you there when they nailed Him to the tree?*
> *Oh! Sometimes it causes me to tremble, tremble, tremble.*
> *Were you there when they nailed Him to the tree?*
>
> AFRICAN-AMERICAN
> SPIRITUAL

Physically, emotionally, spiritually

Physically, the film is harshly stinging and difficult to watch; emotionally, it is absolutely wrenching; spiritually, the message is clear and is driven into one's soul with every excruciating step to the Place of the Skull.

Personally, I will never be the same again! I truly feel reborn!

Christ accepted his own Sacrifice willingly for the salvation of ALL mankind! There is NO GREATER LOVE!!!

❖ Posted on *The Passion of the Christ* website

This movie may change our country

Anticipation

A week before the movie came out my spirit was so stirred. I work at a church and I could feel the anticipation of this movie in the air. We all knew that this movie would be the catapult of personal revival. I knew that I personally would experience revival after seeing this movie.

Silenced

The first Saturday it came out I went with my husband and another couple. My husband had already seen it with our Pastor and Youth Pastor and when he came home at 1am I asked him to tell me about it.

He just told me to go to sleep because he couldn't talk about it. The next morning it was the same. I went to work and I asked the Pastor and Youth Pastor; they

LIGHT *from the* BIBLE

"But he was pierced for our transgressions,
he was crushed for our iniquities;
the punishment that brought us peace was upon him,
and by his wounds we are healed.
We all, like sheep, have gone astray,
each of us has turned to his own way;
and the LORD has laid on him
the iniquity of us all."

ISAIAH 53:5-6

Quotation to ponder

"Jesus became the greatest liar, perjurer, thief, adulterer and murderer that mankind has ever known – not because he committed these sins but because he was actually made sin for us."

MARTIN LUTHER

couldn't talk about it until later that after noon. All they said was it wasn't a movie, that it was a holy experience.

No disappointment

So my expectations were HIGH, and I wasn't disappointed. Mel Gibson did an excellent job on this movie! At the end, as everyone has said, you could hear a pin drop. All you heard were sniffles and silence.

I always knew that Jesus died for me, but it was sterile, not real. This movie gave me a real picture of the gravity of my sins and of how big a price Christ paid for me.

Changed hearts

Thank you Mel Gibson and all who labored. I know you didn't do it for any blessings but you and your family will be blessed.

This movie may change the direction of our country. If not, it will have at least changed the hearts of the millions of Christians. May God Bless you richly!!!

❖ Posted on *The Passion of the Christ* website

Out of my comfort zone

Three points

I have been a Christian living in a comfort zone for many years. When I saw The Passion of the Christ three points jumped off the screen and into my heart:

1. "Love those that persecute you, it is easy to love those that love you. The real reward comes from loving those that are difficult to love."

2. "My heart is ready, Lord." This was so strong, in that we should remain in constant prayer 24/7 as to not miss an opportunity to witness to others. Our hearts should be ready to serve!

3. "Father, forgive them Lord, for they know not what they do." Luke 23:24

❖ Posted on The Passion of the Christ website

LIGHT from the BIBLE

"Blessed are those who are persecuted because of righteousness, for theirs is the kingdom of heaven. Blessed are you when people insult you, persecute you and falsely say all kinds of evil against you because of me."

MATTHEW 5:10-11